CHINESE NEGOTIATING BEHAVIOR

RICHARD H. SOLOMON

CHINESE NEGOTIATING BEHAVIOR

Pursuing Interests Through 'Old Friends'

with an interpretative essay by
Chas. W. Freeman, Jr.

UNITED STATES INSTITUTE OF PEACE PRESS
Washington, D.C.

Cover: (top, left to right) Henry Kissinger, Zhou Enlai, and Mao Zedong (courtesy Chinese Government); (middle) Bill Clinton (left) and Jiang Zemin (AP Photo/Greg Baker); (bottom left) Richard Nixon (left) shaking hands with Zhou Enlai (courtesy Richard Nixon Library); (bottom right) Deng Xiaoping (left) and Jimmy Carter (courtesy Jimmy Carter Library)

United States Institute of Peace
1200 17th Street NW, Suite 200
Washington, DC 20036-3011

New edition first published 1999. Second printing 2001.

Printed in the United States of America

The paper used in this publication meets the minimum requirements of American National Standard for Information Sciences—Permanence of Paper for Printed Library Materials, ANSI Z39.48-1984.

Library of Congress Cataloging-in-Publication Data

Solomon, Richard H., 1937–

Chinese negotiating behavior : pursuing interests through "old friends" / Richard H. Solomon ; with an interpretive essay by Chas. W. Freeman, Jr.

p. cm.

Includes bibliographical references (p.).

ISBN 1-878379-86-0 (paperback : alk. paper)

1. China—Foreign relations—1949– 2. China—Foreign relations—United States. 3. United States—Foreign relations—China. 4. United States—Foreign relations—1945–1989. 5. United States—Foreign relations—1989– 6. Negotiation. 7. Political culture—China. 8. Political psychology—China. I. Title.

DS77.8.S65 1999

99-34937

CIP

Contents

Introduction to the New Edition

The Cold War produced many anomalies in international affairs. Among the more notable, of course, was the superpower-enforced bipolarity, in which ties between nations that may have had a long history of relations were suddenly severed in the global order of opposing alliances. In this world of political and military confrontation and ideological polarization, the United States was cut off for decades from direct dealings with a range of countries, especially in Asia—China, North Korea, Mongolia, North Vietnam. Re-establishing contact after decades of hostility, if not war, was a unique, at times dramatic, and politically momentous process. In the case of the United States and the People's Republic of China, renewing ties after more than twenty years of confrontation was not only a major diplomatic event, but also a strategic maneuver designed to counter a shared security challenge from the Soviet Union.

President Richard Nixon's surprise re-establishment of contact with China in 1971 was carried out through secret diplomacy. Nixon's national security adviser, Henry Kissinger, traveled to Beijing unannounced in the summer of that year to begin a process of "normalizing" relations. Subsequent trips to arrange an agenda before Nixon's historic visit in February 1972 were also conducted in a shroud of secrecy. In the history of diplomacy, this initiative was unique in that Kissinger started out virtually *tabula rasa* in dealing with a country and political system quite different from the Western experience. China was seen as a mysterious and esoteric land on the other side of the world, both literally and figuratively. Bridging this gap—in distance, politics, and culture—became an exercise in exploring differences that were all the more pronounced because of the decades of separation.

A scholar of Western political and diplomatic history, Kissinger found the Chinese in 1971 to be, if not unique, then distinctive in their negotiating behavior. In preparing for his first trip to Beijing (which was done largely without the support of China specialists in the government, out of concern for secrecy), he expected the same kind of confrontational Marxist-Leninist rhetoric he had encountered in negotiations with the Soviets. Those two nations were the leading Communist countries, and the Chinese presumably had learned a great deal about managing negotiations from their colleagues in Moscow before the beginning of the Sino-Soviet rift in 1960. Yet to his surprise, Kissinger discovered that the Chinese employed quite a different negotiating style, dramatically personified in the reception he received from the country's senior political leaders such as Premier Zhou Enlai, a host of top-level foreign ministry officials, and—ultimately—Communist Party Chairman Mao Zedong.

Kissinger's memoirs are replete with almost awestruck recollections of the personal escorts, elaborate tours, and lavish banquets meticulously arranged by his Chinese hosts during his nine visits between 1971 and 1976. And within that relatively brief period, Kissinger found himself characterized as an "old friend" by his new Chinese counterparts. This is not to say that the U.S. national security adviser and, later, secretary of state was unable to assess the intentions of the Chinese behind the veneer of such blandishments and official "friendship," but Kissinger's memoirs reveal not only how enticing he found Chinese diplomacy to be, but also how much he did *not* know during those first encounters about his hosts on the other side of the world—

not only about their negotiating behavior, but more generally their mores, their perceptions, and their conduct with foreigners.

Today, almost thirty years after Kissinger's first, secret trip to Beijing, China remains an esoteric society for most foreigners—whether they are foreign ministry officials, members of trade delegations, or business representatives. Although Kissinger's memoirs provide engrossing *descriptions* of how the Chinese negotiate, there have been relatively few in-depth *analytical* studies of Chinese negotiating behavior. It is in this context that the United States Institute of Peace reprints here my 1995 RAND Corporation study in an attempt to fill that lacuna.

This volume was initially produced to assess the "unique" aspects of Chinese negotiating behavior as perceived by the American officials who encountered the Chinese in the 1970s—after decades of political estrangement. The objective of the study was to better prepare U.S. negotiators for encounters with their unfamiliar and "mysterious" yet reputedly skillful Chinese counterparts. The fundamental assumption of the study was that the relatively isolated Chinese had a distinctive negotiating style. The methodology of the analysis was based on the assumption that the unique aspects of that style would be especially evident to an observer from another culture. In the cultural difference would lie the perception of the uniqueness of, and motivation behind, this distinctive negotiating behavior.

As the following analysis details, the Chinese certainly do evince distinctive negotiating characteristics. Among the more noticeable factors that make a given country's negotiating behavior "distinctive" are physical ambiance, institutional environment, culture (including language, customs, ways of thinking and perceiving), and the personalities of individual negotiators. Each nation possesses distinctive traits in its negotiating technique—for example, the preferred setting and mood, the pressure tactics and manipulative strategies, the pace and the rhythms of the discussions. These characteristics are shaped by the country's history, political institutions, and culture. Nevertheless, practically every nation conducts negotiations according to common "rules" and principles that stem from shared international norms and the fundamental dynamics of a bargaining situation. In the case of the People's Republic of China, all these aspects of the negotiating process—the distinctive and the not-so-distinctive—are explored in this volume.

That said, I should emphasize that "distinctive" is not synonymous with either "unique" or "unfamiliar." Certain negotiating ploys are universal in their utility; others, although given special emphasis by a certain country's negotiators, become comfortably familiar. Some negotiating techniques may be appealing; others, sources of discomfort. This study identifies a number of negotiating tactics that Kissinger found ingratiating and refreshing in the early phases of his discussions with the Chinese. Yet he also came to realize that his gracious hosts were quite practiced in using the crucial elements of time and pressure during the latter phases of a negotiation to attain an agreement that best served their interests.

As this study acknowledges, Kissinger is certainly not the only Western negotiator to have observed distinctive traits in negotiations with the Chinese. Yet he had a unique vantage point from which he could compare the negotiating style of the Chinese with that of many other nations' negotiators he had encountered over the years. Kissinger obviously saw something in the Chinese approach to negotiating that distinguished them from other foreign officials. If he was taken with their effort to establish bonds of "friendship" with representatives of the opposing side, he was equally impressed with another salient technique of the Chinese negotiating style identified in this study—the attempt early in the negotiation to press for commitment to certain fundamental "principles" that both sides could agree upon, and then proceed to bargain on subsidiary issues within the confines of such a mutually agreed upon "principled position."

In a concise comparison of Zhou Enlai with Soviet foreign minister Andrei Gromyko, Kissinger makes clear the distinction he found between the Chinese and Soviet styles of negotiation, going beyond the strong personalities of both men to capture institutional and cultural attributes of their negotiating behavior:

> *Zhou Enlai, possessing the sense of cultural superiority of an ancient civilization, softened the edges of ideological hostility by an insinu-*

> *ating ease of manner and a seemingly effortless skill to penetrate to the heart of the matter. Gromyko, as the spokesman of a country that had never prevailed except by raw power, lacked this confidence; he was obliged to test his mettle in every encounter. It was easy to underestimate him. His bulldozing persistence was a deliberate method of operation, not a gauge of his subtlety.*[1]

All Countries Negotiate in Distinctive Ways

With the end of the Cold War, many countries long separated by the superpower confrontation resumed contacts in efforts to resolve shared problems or develop political and trade relations. Accordingly, many governments that had never negotiated before (U.S.-Mongolia, Japan-Romania, Germany-Vietnam) had their first encounters across the negotiating table. Today, negotiating with culturally and historically unfamiliar counterparts has become commonplace, as political and economic relations expand on a global scale and accelerate with each new technological advance in the telecommunications revolution.

Moreover, with the end of international ideological and political polarization, we live in a time when diplomatic approaches to addressing international problems predominate over the military assertions of power that were characteristic of the colonial era and the Cold War. Not only has the number of countries participating in the international negotiating arena increased dramatically, but also the issues under discussion have become much more diverse and complex. Issues of "low politics" (aid and trade, monetary flows, emigration, environmental disputes) are in many ways much more complicated technical affairs involving many more players than the "high politics" of security agreements and arms control that were dominated by the major powers of the Cold War's opposing camps.

Necessarily, this expansion of the international negotiating environment has created a demand to understand new and unfamiliar negotiating counterparts—to discover the patterns and nuances of unfamiliar negotiating styles. As Chas Freeman's interpretive essay in part two of this new edition makes clear,

---

1. Henry Kissinger, *White House Years,* Boston: Little, Brown, 1979, pp. 792–93.

culture provides for continuity in the distinctive aspects of a country's negotiating behavior, even as diplomats work to adapt their negotiating agendas and styles to a world that is slowly generating certain universal political norms and negotiating procedures, much as French diplomacy created universal diplomatic norms in the seventeenth and eighteenth centuries.

Given the need for understanding the negotiating behavior of many new actors in the international environment, it is surprising that relatively few efforts have been made to give diplomats, policymakers, nongovernmental organizations, and the business community concise "guides" to the negotiating characteristics of particular nations—what to expect of foreign counterparts before, during, and after the formal negotiations on a particular issue have been conducted. After completing this study of Chinese negotiating behavior in the mid-1980s, I urged the U.S. Foreign Service Institute to undertake a series of in-depth comparative assessments of national negotiating behavior. A result of this effort was *National Negotiating Styles,* Hans Binnendijk's 1987 collection of essays on six countries' distinctive negotiating styles. Yet the effort was not sustained; nor did it realize its full analytical potential, in part for lack of a comparative framework of analysis.

Project on Cross-Cultural Negotiation Analysis and Training

The congressional mandate of the United States Institute of Peace is to strengthen the nation's capacity to resolve international conflicts by political means. In partial fulfillment of that commitment, the Institute has established the Cross-Cultural Negotiation (CCN) project—a major, ongoing program of research, publication, and training that assesses through comparative analyses the ways different governments manage the negotiating process. The project is based on the development of a comparative analytical framework for examining different national negotiating styles, and it proceeds on the assumption that culture and institutional differences significantly shape negotiating behavior. The objective of the project is to penetrate the veil of mystery —or at least of unfamiliarity—surrounding different cultures and to remove the uncertainty that can confound American—or other foreign—diplomats and non-governmental negotiators when dealing with unfamiliar countries and counterparts, thus clearing the way for more productive negotiating encounters.

Chinese Negotiating Behavior: Pursuing Interests Through "Old Friends" is thus one of a series of country studies sponsored by the Institute. It joins Jerrold Schecter's *Russian Negotiating Behavior: Continuity and Transition* and forthcoming studies by Scott Snyder, Michael Blaker, and Richard Smyser of North Korean, Japanese, and German negotiating behavior, respectively. Underlying these country-oriented assessments are two interpretive works published by the Institute that are designed to systematically explore the proposition that culture plays a significant role in shaping negotiating behavior—Raymond Cohen's *Negotiating Across Cultures: International Communication in an Interdependent World,* and Kevin Avruch's *Culture and Conflict Resolution.*

In addition, the CCN project and the body of research that is emerging from it are designed not just to establish an analytical framework and comparative database, but also to provide the material for training practitioners, enhancing their cross-cultural negotiating skills, and helping them formulate more effective procedures and strategies for managing specific negotiations.

Background of the Chinese Case Study

I want to express appreciation to the RAND Corporation for the rights to reprint as part of the Institute's series on national negotiating styles the public version of this study, published by RAND in 1995 under the title *Chinese Political Negotiating Behavior, 1967–1984.*

The RAND study originated as a classified analysis of Chinese negotiating behavior commissioned by the U.S. government in 1983, when I was on the staff of the RAND Corporation. I was the study's principal investigator because of my familiarity with the negotiating record—having been a member of Henry Kissinger's China team at the National Security Council during the early years of U.S. efforts to normalize relations with the People's Republic. Because the analysis drew heavily on the official, classified negotiating record, distribution of the study was originally restricted to government officials, although RAND published an unclassified summary of the findings in 1985.

In 1994, the *Los Angeles Times* filed a Freedom of Information Act suit that led to a federal court decision ordering declassification of most of the 1985 study. In 1995, RAND decided to publish the declassified portions of the original study, in the words of RAND senior vice president Michael D. Rich's preface to that edition, "because of the analytical and historical value of the work, and because of the continuing interest to the United States of managing effectively a relationship with a major country that is likely to be of even greater significance in world affairs in the coming century."

With the passage of more than a decade since the study was completed, it is fair to ask whether the analytical findings from the original study have become dated. In order to assess the degree of continuity or change in Chinese negotiating behavior, we asked Ambassador Chas Freeman, a career Foreign Service officer with more than three decades of experience in dealing with the Chinese, to evaluate the ways in which Chinese negotiating behavior has, and has not, changed since the original study was conducted. As Ambassador Freeman notes in his essay included in this edition, while the People's Republic has undergone tremendous political, economic, and social changes in the post-Mao era, one facet of contemporary Chinese behavior in the international realm that remains remarkably durable is their negotiating technique. "Fifteen years after Dick Solomon first published his analysis as a classified document, his conclusions have lost none of their force and utility. . . . With respect to the fundamentals of the Chinese negotiating practices he describes," Ambassador Freeman concludes, "it seems fair to say: *plus ça change, plus c'est la même chose.*"

The analysis in the pages that follow elaborates on the sources, elements, and nuances of that negotiating style.

PART ONE

memcons- memoranda/conversation

Summary

This study of Chinese political negotiating behavior assesses patterns and practices in the ways officials of the People's Republic of China (PRC) managed high-level political negotiations with the United States during the "normalization" phase of relations between the two countries. It is designed to provide guidance for senior American officials prior to their first negotiating encounters with PRC counterparts and to establish control over the documentary record of U.S.-PRC political exchanges between 1967 and 1984.

This assessment is based on analysis of the official negotiating record of U.S.-PRC exchanges during this period (the memoranda of conversation—"memcons"—and reporting cables that document formal exchanges), interviews with more than thirty U.S. officials who have conducted political negotiations with the Chinese, and such additional materials as the memoirs of former senior U.S. government officials, Chinese press statements, and official PRC documentation.

The basic finding of this study is that Chinese officials conduct negotiations in a distinctive, but not unique, manner consisting of a highly organized and meticulously managed progression of well-defined stages. It is an approach influenced by both Western diplomatic practice and the Marxist-Leninist tradition acquired from the Soviet Union and through dealings with the international communist movement. Its fundamental style and most distinctive qualities, however, are based on China's own cultural tradition and political practices.

The most distinctive characteristic of Chinese negotiating behavior is the effort to develop and manipulate strong interpersonal relationships with foreign officials—a pattern termed here "the games of *guanxi*," or relationship games. This approach to politics is shaped by China's Confucian political tradition. The Chinese distrust impersonal or legalistic negotiations. Thus, in managing a negotiation they attempt to identify a sympathetic counterpart official in a foreign government and work to cultivate a personal relationship, a sense of "friendship" *(you-yi)* and obligation; they then attempt to manipulate feelings of good will, obligation, guilt, or dependence to achieve their negotiating objectives. The frequently used term "friendship" implies to the Chinese a strong sense of obligation for the "old friend" to provide support and assistance to China.

The Negotiating Process

American officials have characterized negotiations with the PRC as a linear process of sequential and relatively discrete stages which unfold as the two sides explore issues of common concern. This process is illustrated in the table on page 5.

Opening Moves

PRC officials make a determined effort at the outset of a negotiation to establish a sympathetic counterpart official as an interlocutor, to cultivate a personal relationship (friendship) with him; they press for the acceptance of their principles as the basis of the relationship. They also seek to structure a negotiating agenda favorable to their objectives.

The Chinese view a political negotiation as reconciling the principles and objectives of the two sides and testing the other government's commitment to a relationship with the PRC. They do *not* see it as a highly technical process of haggling over

The Linear Process of PRC Political Negotiations

(1) → **Opening Moves**	(2) → **Period of Assessment**	(3) → **End Game**	(4) → **Implementation**
• Establish a relationship with a "friendly" counterpart official • Establish a favorable agenda • Gain commitment to PRC "principles"	• Draw out interlocutor • Apply pressures • Test intentions, patience	• Conclude an agreement, or • Reserve position, or • Abort the negotiation	• Press for adherence • Make additional demands

details, in which the two sides initially table maximum positions and then move to a point of convergence through incremental compromises.

To establish a framework for a relationship, PRC officials will press their counterparts at the outset of a negotiation to accept certain general "principles" (such as those embodied in the Shanghai Communiqué of 1972). Such political ground rules are then used to constrain the interlocutor's bargaining flexibility as the negotiation proceeds and to test the sincerity of his desire to develop and sustain a relationship with China. Experience shows, however, that when a PRC negotiator wants to reach an accord, he can set aside the emphasis on principles and reach a concrete agreement that may appear to have little relationship to the principles that were seemingly essential early in the negotiation.

Period of Assessment

Chinese officials are skilled in protracting a negotiation to explore the limits of their adversary's views, flexibility, and patience. They will resist exposing their own position until their counterparts' stand is fully known and their endurance has been well tested.

Facilitating maneuvers. The Chinese try to conduct negotiations on their own territory, as this gives them maximum control over the ambience of official exchanges. They seek to establish a positive mood through meticulous orchestration of hospitality (cuisine, sightseeing, etc.), media play, banquet toasts, and protocol. They may attempt to minimize confrontation or differences of view through subtle and indirect presentation of their positions. They may communicate difficult messages through trusted intermediaries. And when they seek to avoid the breakdown of a negotiation, they may resort to stalling tactics or reach a partial agreement while reserving their own position on important issues on which they do not wish to compromise.

Pressure tactics. PRC officials will resort to a variety of tactics to put an interlocutor on the defensive and make him feel he has minimal control over the negotiating process. They are skilled at making a foreign counterpart appear to be the supplicant or *demandeur* in the relationship. They play political adversaries against each other and may alternate hard and accommodating moods by shifting from "bad guy" to "good guy" officials. They may urge a foreign negotiator to accommodate to their position using the argument that if he does not, his "friends" in the PRC leadership will be weakened by failure to reach agreement. And they tend to put pressure on a sympathetic counterpart negotiator on the assumption that a "friend" will make a special effort to repair problems in the relationship.

The Chinese often present themselves as the injured party, seeking to shame an interlocutor with recitation of faults on the part of his government or his failure to live up to past agreements or to the "spirit" of mutually accepted principles. They are meticulous record-keepers and will hold a negotiator responsible for his past words and the commitments of his predecessors. They are skilled at using the press to create public pressures on a foreign negotiating team. And they may seek to trap a negotiator against a time deadline (so that he must make decisions under pressure).

The essential quality of Chinese pressure tactics is to make the foreign negotiator, with whom they have gone to some lengths to develop a personal, or "friendly," association, feel that his positive relationship with China is in jeopardy, that he has not done enough to warrant being considered an "old friend," and that he must do more for the relationship to justify Chinese support and good will. It is this tension of the relationship game that gives dealings with the Chinese much of their distinctive quality.

End Game

When PRC officials believe that they have tested the limits of their negotiating counterparts' position and that a formal understanding serves their interests, they can move rapidly to conclude an agreement.

They may let a negotiation appear to deadlock to test their interlocutor's patience and firmness, then have a senior leader intervene to cut the knot of the apparent deadlock. Agreements are usually reached at the very last moment of a negotiating encounter—or even just after a deadline has passed. Once Chinese leaders have decided to reach an agreement, their negotiators can be quite flexible in working out concrete arrangements.

Implementation

Chinese officials assess the manner in which a counterpart government implements an agreement as a sign of how seriously or sincerely that government views its relationship with the PRC. They press for strict implementation of all understandings and they are quick to find fault.

At the same time, Chinese officials sometimes give the impression that agreements are never quite final. They will seek modifications of understandings when it serves their purposes; and the conclusion of an agreement is the occasion for pressing the counterpart government for new concessions. If they are unable to fully implement an agreement themselves, however, they will ask the counterpart to "understand" their difficulties on the basis of friendship, or they will make excuses that put the burden of responsibility on the other party.

Discussion

Reflecting the workings of the relationship game, American negotiators describe their dealings with the Chinese as at once elating and frustrating. PRC officials can establish a positive mood when they want to build a constructive relationship; and they impress their U.S. counterparts as personally attractive, highly competent individuals with whom it is easy to deal at a human level. On the other hand, Chinese officials—who consider themselves the representatives of a once and future great power—can adopt a self-righteous and lecturing air, presuming the right to criticize their "friends" (while being highly defensive of their own positions) and requiring that negotiations be conducted on their own terms.

The experience of countries that have established highly interdependent relations with the PRC has demonstrated that the Chinese can be highly demanding and manipulative of those on whom they have established a dependent relationship (as was the case with the "elder brother" Soviet Union in the 1950s), or self-righteously assertive in dealing with those who have established a subordinate relationship with them (as was the case with Albania in the 1960s).

Guidelines for Dealing with PRC Counterparts

This analysis suggests the following "lessons learned" that U.S. officials should keep in mind if they are to be more effective in dealing with PRC counterparts:

Know the substantive issues cold. Chinese officials are meticulous in preparing for negotiating sessions, and their staffs are very effective in briefing them on technical issues. They will use any indication of sloppy preparation against an interlocutor.

Master the past negotiating record. PRC officials have full control over the prior negotiating record, and they do not hesitate to use it to pressure a counterpart.

Know your own bottom line. A clear sense of the objectives of a negotiation will enable a U.S. official to avoid being trapped in commitments to general principles and to resist Chinese efforts to drag out a negotiation. Incremental compromises suggest to the Chinese that their interlocutor's final position has not yet been reached.

Present your position in a broad framework. The Chinese seem to find it easier to compromise on specific issues if they have a sense of the broader purposes of their interlocutor in developing a relationship with the PRC. They distrust quick deals, and they appreciate presentations that suggest seriousness of purpose and an interest in maintaining a long-term relationship with China.

Be patient. Do not expect quick or easy agreement. A Chinese negotiator will have trouble convincing his superiors that he has fully tested the limits of his counterpart's position if he has not protracted the discussions. Assume you will be subjected to unexplained delays and various forms of pressure to test your resolve.

Avoid time deadlines. Resist negotiating in circumstances where you must have agreement by a certain date. The Chinese will assume that your urgency to conclude a deal can be played to their advantage.

Minimize media pressures. PRC negotiators use public expectations about a negotiation to pressure their interlocutors. Confidential handling of negotiating exchanges, the disciplining of leaks, and the minimizing of press exposure are taken by the Chinese as signs of seriousness of purpose. Negotiation via the press will evoke a sharp Chinese response.

Understand the PRC political context and the style of your Chinese interlocutor. Despite the difficulties of assessing the domestic PRC political scene, an evaluation of internal factional pressures and the style of your counterparts will help in understanding Chinese objectives and the limits of their negotiating flexibility, as well as in reading the signals or loaded language of a very different culture and political system.

Understand the Chinese meaning of *friendship*. Know that the Chinese expect a lot of their "friends." Resist the flattery of being an "old friend" or the sentimentality that Chinese hospitality readily evokes. Do not promise more than you can deliver, but expect that you will be pressured to honor past commitments. Resist Chinese efforts to shame or play on guilt feelings for presumed errors or shortcomings.

Develop a strategic orientation to dealing with the Chinese. The blandishments of the friendship game and Chinese pressure tactics are most effectively defended against by developing a strategic orientation suited to American negotiating practices and objectives. An attitude of restrained openness and interest in identifying and working to attain common objectives is the best protection against Chinese efforts to maneuver the foreign negotiator into the position of *demandeur* or supplicant.

Parry Chinese pressure tactics in order to maintain control over the negotiating process. Chinese negotiating tactics are readily understandable and, in some measure, even predictable. Therefore, U.S. negotiators should develop countertactics that will parry PRC maneuvers and will demonstrate competence and control over the negotiating process. Tactical manipulations applied in excess or for their own sake, however, are likely to erode confidence and undermine the credibility of a negotiation.

Acknowledgments

I am indebted to David Gries, who, in his role as National Intelligence Officer for East Asia, conceived and supported this project; and to James McCullough, Director of East Asian Analysis, for the support his office provided throughout the research effort.

Many officials and former officials of the U.S. government gave generously of their time in the interviews that were a major source of information and insight for this study. Other officials contributed in important ways to the assembling of the documentary record of U.S.-PRC negotiations. I particularly want to express appreciation for the support and assistance of Assistant to the President for National Security Affairs Robert C. McFarlane; David Laux, Brenda Reger, and Donna Sirko of the National Security Council staff; Assistant Secretary of State Paul D. Wolfowitz; Executive Secretary of the Department of State M. Charles Hill; and Elijah Kelly, Jr., of the Executive Secretariat. Henry A. Kissinger and General Brent Scowcroft were helpful in enabling me to gain access to the records of the Nixon and Ford administrations. And Professor Michel Oksenberg assisted in assembling the key documents from the Carter administration.

Intellectual stimulation for this project has come from numerous sources, but I particularly want to express my indebtedness to Dr. Steven R. Pieczenik for his insights into the negotiating process (in particular, for his suggestions on negotiating counter-strategies); to Professor Lucian W. Pye of the Massachusetts Institute of Technology, whose parallel study of Chinese commercial negotiating behavior[1] provided many interpretive insights and an intellectual foil for this study of political negotiating behavior; and to Charles Neuhauser for his assessments of Chinese politics and U.S.-PRC relations.

Anna Sun Ford provided timely and ever-productive research assistance for the project, and my secretary Mary Yanokawa is due special credit not only for typing this and the other manuscripts of this project, but also for organizing my work effort and providing professional support throughout the project.

---

1. Lucian W. Pye, *Chinese Commercial Negotiating Style,* Cambridge, Mass.: Oelgeschlager, Gunn & Hain, 1982.

1

Introduction

Objectives of the Study

The analysis presented here is part of a study undertaken to provide supporting materials for operational officials and analysts of the U.S. government concerned with interpreting and managing relations with the People's Republic of China (PRC). The primary objective of this project has been to analyze the way Chinese officials manage political negotiations by drawing on the official record and the experiences of U.S. officials who have dealt with PRC counterparts during the phase of Sino-American relations in which both governments tried to break out of two decades of confrontation to normalize the relationship.

This study is summarized in a briefing analysis designed to provide information for senior officials of the U.S. government prior to their first negotiating encounters with Chinese counterparts (Solomon, 1985). These two volumes provide an analytical assessment of one of the most interesting episodes in America's post–World War II foreign relations: the effort to move from a long period of political rivalry and military confrontation with the PRC—"Red China" or "Communist China," as it was termed during the 1950s and 1960s—to a relationship in which the two countries could eliminate the hostility of the Cold War era, manage continuing differences over the future of Taiwan in a nonconfrontational manner, and cooperate in limited measure in dealing with shared international political and security problems, primarily the military threat to both countries from the Soviet Union.

Sources of Data: Memoranda of Conversation, Interviews, and Memoirs

The primary source of data upon which this analysis is based is the official record of negotiating exchanges between senior U.S. officials and their PRC counterparts—the memoranda of conversation, or "memcons," which are the basic documentary record of intergovernmental negotiations. A secondary source is the reporting cables by which State Department negotiators document the results of negotiations conducted in the field under formal instructions.

Because the paper record gives only a partial sense of the negotiating experience, the author also conducted interviews with more than thirty senior American officials who had negotiated with Chinese counterparts during the years covered in this study —beginning with officials of the Nixon administration and running through officials of the Carter and Reagan administrations. These officials had managed the negotiations on normalization and the August 17, 1982, Joint Communiqué on the issue of American arms sales to Taiwan.

To gain a comparative perspective on Chinese negotiating practices, the author also interviewed six officials from agencies other than the Department of State who conducted negotiations with PRC officials during the past twelve years, and several U.S. businessmen who have had considerable experience in commercial negotiations with PRC state trading organizations. In addition, the author drew heavily on insights into Chinese commercial negotiating practices contained in a RAND study based on intensive interviews with American, Japanese, and Hong Kong businessmen that was carried out, in part, to provide a basis of comparison between political and commercial negotiating practices (see Pye, 1982).

It should also be mentioned that the author of this study participated directly in political negotiations with the Chinese during his tenure as a staff member of the National Security Council (NSC) between 1971 and 1976. This experience and his subsequent involvement in China policy matters as a RAND consultant to the NSC and the Departments of Defense and State provided direct exposure to Chinese negotiating practices and to the official record, as well as personal familiarity with the senior American officials interviewed for this project.

In addition, selected secondary source materials and studies—historical analyses of pre-Communist Chinese negotiating practices, and memoirs of the senior U.S. officials who conducted negotiations with PRC counterparts during the 1960s, 1970s, and 1980s—provided further information and insights into the manner in which Chinese officials seek to manage the negotiating process.

Chinese Negotiating Behavior: Distinctive, but Not Unique; Purposeful, if Not Fully Planned

> Henry Kissinger: *Many visitors have come to this beautiful, and to us, mysterious land. . . .*
>
> Zhou Enlai (interrupting): *You will not find it mysterious. When you have become familiar with it, it will not be as mysterious as before.*[1]

This study was undertaken, in part, to demystify dealings with a country that has long been viewed in the West as mysterious and esoteric. The sense of mystery surrounding China reflects, in part, the distance that Chinese officials have tried to maintain since imperial times between their country and often-threatening foreign "barbarians"; it also reflects the significant differences in culture and language that continue to separate East from West, as well as the great chasm of ideology and history that further divided the

---

1. Zhou-Kissinger, July 9, 1971. Excerpts from the official negotiating exchanges are referenced in this volume by the officials involved and the date of the exchange. Chinese given and place names are spelled in the *pin-yin* system of Romanization, adopted by the PRC as its official system in 1979.

PRC and the United States during the post–Korean War decades when the two countries confronted each other as enemies.

From today's perspective, it is perhaps difficult to recall the sense of the unknown that surrounded the inception of the Sino-American normalization dialogue in 1971. Henry Kissinger's remark to Zhou Enlai about the mysteriousness of his country (quoted above), made during their first encounter, evokes only a bit of the flavor of the national security adviser's secret trip to a country with which the United States had had almost no direct dealings since 1949. Yet Zhou's retort to Kissinger—that familiarity would demystify China in the eyes of yet another generation of somewhat awed foreigners—has proved to be accurate. The negotiating record of the period covered by this study reveals patterns of behavior and a Chinese approach to managing negotiations that are both comprehensible and, in surprising measure, predictable. As we will describe throughout this study, the negotiating behavior of PRC officials is consistent, and despite their occasional efforts to present an obscure or deceptive face to the outside world, their actions are readily interpretable (at least in hindsight).

One of the objectives of this project is to forearm U.S. negotiating officials and analysts of the PRC political scene with a sense of how the Chinese manage the negotiating process that will enable U.S. negotiators to interpret with greater accuracy the often subtle political signals that are part of that process.

It is also important at the outset to make two fundamental interpretive points which, for the sake of presentational brevity, will not be repeated endlessly throughout this report. First, despite the distinctive quality or "flavor" of dealings with the Chinese, many—if not most—of their negotiating practices are not unique. Many of the facilitating maneuvers and pressure tactics PRC negotiators use are also encountered in dealings with other countries, although the particular style or intensity may be different elsewhere. In short, there is much that is universal in the negotiating process; and the Chinese, for all that is distinctive about their culture, have not developed a unique approach to conducting negotiations.

Yet most of the American officials interviewed for this study did say that the Chinese conducted negotiations in a distinctive manner. Kissinger was impressed with the "principled stand" Chinese officials assumed at the outset of his dealings with them, and with their sense of the importance of the credibility of their word, which led them to "eschew the petty maneuvers that characterized . . . negotiations with other communists" (Kissinger, 1979, p. 744). From his first negotiating session with PRC Vice Foreign Minister Huang Hua in the summer of 1971, Kissinger learned that the Chinese preferred not to negotiate by beginning with an initially exaggerated position from which they moved only slowly in "salami-slicing" fashion; rather, they preferred "to determine as well as possible [at the outset] the nature of a reasonable solution, get there in one jump, and then stick to that position" (Kissinger, 1979, p. 753). As Kissinger recalled in his memoirs:

> *Huang Hua . . . suggested that we put aside the drafting and each tell the other frankly what his needs were. . . . We spent two hours on this [and after some further delay] . . . Huang Hua presented a draft . . . so close to our needs that we could accept it with a change of only one word. (Kissinger, 1979, p. 752)*[2]

Kissinger said he so preferred this style of negotiating that he subsequently sought to use it in his dealings with other governments:

> *The strategy of getting in one jump to a defensible position defines the irreducible position unambiguously; it is easier to defend than the cumulative impact over a long period of a series of marginal moves in which process always threatens to dominate substance. (Kissinger, 1979, p. 752)*

The second basic interpretive point is that while the Chinese conduct negotiations in a purposeful and meticulously planned manner, they are not always in control of the process and often "feel their way" in situations they do not fully understand. The analysis reported here may, upon occasion, make it appear as if the Chinese are almost superhuman in their ability to plan and manipulate a negotiating situation. The record does not show this to be the case, although the analytical process, by its

2. See also Kissinger's nostalgic recollection of his first encounter with PRC negotiators in the summer of 1971, expressed during a dinner with Vice Foreign Minister Qiao Guanhua on November 13, 1972 (Kissinger, 1979).

very nature, extracts from a more complex reality the patterns of behavior that comprise the Chinese approach to negotiating. There *are* distinct and repetitive patterns in Chinese negotiating behavior, and American negotiators should draw confidence from the fact that their PRC counterparts will conduct negotiations in a relatively predictable manner, one that has been dealt with effectively by other U.S. officials in pursuit of American policy objectives.

China's Response to the West: Three Sources of PRC Negotiating Style

The American experience in dealing with the Chinese over a century and a half—since presidential envoy Caleb Cushing negotiated the Treaty of Nanking in 1844—indicates that Chinese negotiating behavior has evolved over time and in changing circumstances in response to two major sources of pressure: (1) the impact of the Western countries that established, by threat and use of force, the treaty port system that endured into the mid-twentieth century; and (2) the Marxist-Leninist experience absorbed by the Chinese political elite through both Kuomintang and (certainly more intensely) Communist dealings with the Soviet Union and the International Communist Movement.[3]

American students of China's nineteenth-century attempts to adjust to Western pressures have documented the Qing Dynasty's efforts to learn enough Western law and negotiating practice to turn the intrusive foreigners' sources of power back on them in the service of protecting the integrity of the traditional imperial system.[4] Beginning in the 1860s, both Manchu and Han officials reluctantly began to translate Western books, sought ways of absorbing foreign military technology to strengthen the

3. This complex history, well documented in the academic literature, will not be reviewed here. It should be remembered, however, that not only did the Chinese Communist party have extensive dealings with the Soviet Union—where many of its leading cadre were trained—but the Kuomintang or Nationalists did as well. Both Chiang Kai-shek and his son Chiang Ching-kuo had periods of training in the USSR.

4. See, in particular, Eastman (1967), Hsu (1960), and Fairbank and Teng (1954).

dynasty's defenses, and began to send students abroad to learn Western ways.

This process of adapting to a wider world continues today, in China's current efforts to modernize itself, to tap the sources of wealth and power that enabled the West to intrude upon the Middle Kingdom—yet without compromising the essence of China's own culture and social imperatives. Once again, China is sending a generation of students abroad to learn foreign languages, science, and management techniques; and Chinese diplomats are gradually adapting to foreign conventions—as symbolized by PRC officials shedding the Mao suits they wore at the beginning of the normalization process and adopting contemporary Western attire.

The second major source of foreign influence on Beijing's diplomatic practice was the Chinese Communist party's six decades of contact with other socialist states and parties—particularly the Soviet Union. America's post-1949 dealings with Communist China were with a country closely allied to the USSR and a political elite strongly influenced by the Marxist-Leninist style of diplomacy practiced by Moscow's envoys.[5] The writings of the American negotiators who faced Chinese counterparts at Panmunjom, Geneva, and Warsaw during the 1950s and 1960s reveal a frustrating experience closely akin to that endured by other U.S. officials in negotiating encounters with Soviet diplomats. Beijing's use of "adversarial" negotiating techniques was vividly described by one of the participants in the Warsaw ambassadorial exchanges (and provides so striking a contrast to Kissinger's experience with many of these same officials a decade later that it is hard to believe the two men are describing the same country):

> *Across the table, the Chinese Communist negotiator sits cold and taut as a steel spring, sternly unapproachable, suspicious, impenetrable, a rigidly disciplined agent reading his lines with mechanical precision. He is able, persistent, imperturbable—and frustratingly*

5. A particularly useful historical review of Soviet negotiating practice is U.S. House, Committee on Foreign Affairs (1979).

> *predictable in style. Negotiation with him is an ordeal, for he makes it so.* (Young, 1968, p. 338)

The Chinese evidently had learned from Moscow the use of the negotiating process as a weapon in the revolutionary struggle. The memoirs of Admiral Turner Joy; Ambassadors Arthur Dean, U. Alexis Johnson, and Jacob Beam; and the others who conducted negotiations in the 1950s with the Chinese Communists (a number of whom, including Zhou Enlai, Ye Jianying, Huang Hua, Zhang Wenjin, Pu Shouchang, and Ji Chaozhu, were also our primary counterparts in the normalization process) recount a suspiciousness, a use of invective, an inclination to struggle tenaciously over the formulation of an agenda, skillful use of the mass media to build pressures on an adversary government, and other combative tactics that seem right out of Moscow's playbook.

Perhaps the most vivid account of the use of negotiations as an extension of revolutionary warfare is contained in Mao Zedong's description of the Chinese Communist party's strategy for dealing with the Kuomintang on the eve of the final phase of the Civil War:

> *How to give "tit-for-tat" [literally, to struggle at opposed spearpoints] depends on the situation. Sometimes not going to negotiations is tit-for-tat; and sometimes going for negotiations is also tit-for-tat. We were right not to before, also right this time . . . for we exploded the rumor spread by the Kuomintang that the Communist Party did not want peace and unity. . . . They were totally unprepared, and we had to make all the proposals. As a result of the negotiations, the Kuomintang has accepted the general policy of peace and unity. That's fine. If the Kuomintang launches civil war again, it will put itself in the wrong in the eyes of the whole nation and the whole world, and we shall have all the more reason to smash its attacks by a war of self-defense.* (Mao, 1965, p. 56)

A third, and possibly the most enduring, influence on PRC negotiating behavior is China's own cultural tradition and historical experience. The Western diplomats who first encountered officials of the Qing Dynasty described a highly ritualized negotiating process derived from the old tribute system in which the foreign emissary was escorted to the Chinese capital by specially designated officials, subjected to exquisite hospitality and plied with gifts (even as his physical movements were highly restricted), and then subjected to alternations of pressure and accommodation. As one historian of this period described it:

> *The mistrust with which the barbarians were viewed crystallized into a policy of segregation and of constant watchfulness and precaution when they had to be admitted into China. . . . Envoys were escorted . . . over an assigned route to and from Peking . . . lest they make trouble or become too wise. They were not allowed to roam about freely in the streets without first securing permission from the proper Chinese authority, who would then specially guard the streets they were to pass through. Westerners who came to China for trade were carefully quarantined in . . . the city of Canton. (Hsu, 1960, p. 10)*

This pattern of diplomatic practices was still evident in the way Kissinger was treated during his first negotiating encounters with PRC officials and in the isolation of the foreign business community in Canton until the late 1970s.

There is also an underlying dynamic to the contemporary Chinese negotiating process that seems to tap the fundamental roots of China's cultural pattern: an effort to draw the foreign negotiator into a personal relationship, establish ties of friendship, and then subject him to all the blandishments and pressures that are basic to the Chinese social order. While one sees certain elements of Western and Soviet political practice in contemporary PRC management of the negotiating process, the Chinese instinctively seek to enmesh the foreign negotiator in the same web of attractions and pressures that operate in their own society and political system.

The foreign observer can see in curious combination the contemporary workings of these three sources of influence on PRC political negotiating style. On the one hand, most American diplomats have been impressed by the straightforward, nonideological manner in which they can discuss issues with their PRC counterparts. The rhetoric of Marxism-Leninism never enters into the official dialogue. Yet we know well from the official press that the Chinese discuss policy issues among themselves in classic Marxist-Leninist fashion—imputing to foreign adversaries motives and objectives that are basic to the rhetoric of the Communist movement. At the same time, political polemics are often conducted in the Chinese press in the terms of historical analogies, as if the figures of ancient dynasties are still relevant to China's contemporary circumstances (see Liberthal, 1977). It is this essential core of "Chineseness" that gives negotiating encounters with the PRC their distinctive character.

Phases in the Evolution of U.S.-PRC Relations

If there is an enduring "Chineseness" to PRC negotiating behavior, there is also an evident variability in the way Chinese Communist authorities have conducted their relations with the United States. As noted earlier, the American negotiators who dealt with PRC officials during the 1950s and 1960s experienced a very different negotiating process from that faced by the officials who attempted to normalize U.S.-PRC relations during the 1970s. This variability in style is presumably based on the highly context-dependent quality of Chinese social behavior, which has been noted by anthropologists and other analysts of the Chinese tradition,[6] as well as on China's continuing effort to learn and adapt to unfamiliar foreign ways. For purposes of this study, it is perhaps sufficient to note that there are significant differences in style and emotional mood associated with the various time phases in the Sino-American relationship.

In the broadest terms, we can identify four distinct periods in America's dealings with the Chinese Communists. The initial period of official contact began in the late 1930s and ran through World War II and the subsequent civil war years, when the Chinese Communists were an insurgent political and military movement seeking American support for their efforts during the "War of Resistance" to harass Japan's occupation forces in China (and, in the process, to undercut U.S. support for the Nationalist government of Chiang Kai-shek). During this period, official contact was first established through the Communist mission in the Nationalist wartime capital of Chungking (headed by Zhou Enlai), then developed via the U.S. Army's Dixie Mission to the Communist headquarters at Yanan, and later maintained through the

6. On this aspect of Chinese social behavior, see Weakland (1950) and Whyte (1974).

mediation mission of General George C. Marshall, who tried to prevent the outbreak of full-scale civil war between the Nationalists and the Communists in late 1945 and early 1946.

The second period, from 1949 to 1969, began with the Communist victory in the civil war and the concurrent breakdown in official U.S.-PRC contacts, followed by the turn to confrontation during the Korean War and the near-fruitless series of negotiations conducted between the two governments over the ensuing two decades—at Panmunjom in 1953, at the Geneva Conference on Indochina in 1954 (when Secretary of State John Foster Dulles refused to shake hands with Zhou Enlai), at the subsequent ambassadorial talks at Geneva (from 1955 to 1957, during which one agreement—a prisoner exchange—was negotiated), and at the Warsaw talks, which continued without result until early 1970, when both sides, in the first moves toward the normalization dialogue of the 1970s, agreed to establish direct, high-level political contacts.

The third phase, the normalization effort, formally began with the 135th and 136th Warsaw talks in January and February 1970 and came to world attention after the announcement of National Security Adviser Henry Kissinger's secret visit to Beijing in July 1971. This phase continued through subsequent public Kissinger trips to China and the visits of President Nixon in 1972 and President Ford in late 1975, and concluded with the establishment of diplomatic relations at the end of 1978, after six months of quiet negotiations conducted in Beijing by U.S. Liaison Office Chief Leonard Woodcock.

The fourth phase, while not representing as sharp a break in pattern as did the changes between the earlier periods, began in January 1979 with mutual diplomatic recognition and the exchange of ambassadors and includes the full institutionalization of the U.S.-PRC relationship (the signing of various treaties and formal trade agreements, the evolution of a legal infrastructure for management of trade and cultural exchanges, etc.). This period also includes the political negotiations conducted during 1981 and 1982 to establish ground rules for handling the issue of American arms sales to Taiwan.

The study reported here focuses on the third and fourth periods in the relationship. It describes the pattern of negotiating behavior in circumstances where the Chinese Communist authorities had decided that their interests would be served by constructing a positive relationship with the United States.[7]

---

7. An interesting question, which we do not attempt to answer in this analysis, is how useful the insights about PRC negotiating behavior gained from the normalization record might be if the relationship should, at some future time, deteriorate into a new period of confrontation.

2

The Context

The Chinese negotiating style reflects the influence of a cultural tradition that is only vaguely familiar to most Americans. To a remarkable degree, the Chinese seem able to suffuse the negotiation process with an atmosphere and a dynamic that are projections of their social system. PRC officials bring to encounters with their American counterparts a worldview shaped by their country's long imperial past, and they instinctively seek to manage negotiations in ways that draw on the patterns of interpersonal relations of a collectivist society that, over the centuries, has developed a refined and highly ritualized style of managing social and political relationships.

This chapter sketches the cultural and institutional context within which negotiations with the Chinese take place: Chinese attitudes toward, and approaches to dealing with, an unfamiliar and often threatening world beyond China; the remarkable capacity of the Chinese to establish and manipulate personal relationships with foreign officials in a way that is a clear projection of Chinese social practices; and the bureaucratic and political context within which the PRC negotiating official operates.

Zhou Enlai *(right)* greets Henry Kissinger during a visit to Beijing in 1971. *(Courtesy Chinese Government)*

Deng Xiaoping *(left)* meets former president Richard Nixon in Beijing in 1985. *(AP Photo/Neal Ulevich)*

Deng Xiaoping tries on a western-style hat during a visit to Houston in 1979. *(AP/Wide World Photos)*

Deng Xiaoping dines at the home of Zbigniew Brzezinski, President Carter's national security adviser, January 1979. *Left to right:* Michel Oksenberg, Zhang Wenjin, Richard Holbrooke, Mme. Zuo Lin, Cyrus Vance, Deng, Ji Chao Zhu, Brzezinski. *(Courtesy of the White House)*

China in the World: The Ambivalences of a Former Imperial Power

Much of China's difficulty in adapting to the modern world seems related to the tradition of a culturally homogeneous and insular peasant empire that for centuries considered itself *Zhong Guo,* or the Middle Kingdom—the cultural center of the known world, which the Chinese tried to control through a tributary system of relations with such bordering kingdoms as Korea, Indochina, and Burma.

Contemporary Chinese leaders are painfully aware of the constraints their country's social traditions place on their efforts to promote modernization—even as they assume that China, with its great imperial past, will once again establish itself, by a kind of natural right as well as by accomplishment, as a major world power. In a 1973 conversation with Henry Kissinger, Communist Party Chairman Mao Zedong—in a relaxed and reflective mood following the signing of the Paris accords on the Vietnam War —commented on the "feudal ideas" of his people, and their aversion to foreign ways:

> *The Chinese are very alien-excluding. For instance, in your country you can let in so many nationalities, yet in China how many foreigners do you see? . . . You have about 600,000 Chinese in the United States. We probably don't even have 60 Americans here. . . . I don't know why the Chinese never like foreigners. . . . There are no Indians perhaps. . . . In the past the Chinese went abroad and they didn't want to learn the local language. . . . You know Chinese are very obstinate and conservative.*[1]

This innate conservatism and aversion to foreign ways are reinforced by the Chinese belief that for more than a century they have been humiliated and mistreated by imperialistic or hegemonic powers of the West—a mix of attitudes and emotions that underlies a self-righteous sense that China has been denied its proper place in the world and that the countries that formerly mistreated China owe it a debt. This theme is stressed by PRC

1. Mao-Kissinger, February 17–18, 1973.

officials with their American counterparts in, for example, discussions of the Taiwan issue.[2]

China's search for a way out of its imperial backwardness that will not jeopardize its own sense of identity embodies much of the anguish and drama of the country's internal politics and foreign relations since the late nineteenth century. China's first "turn to the West," beginning with the "self-strengthening" movement of the 1860s and reaching a peak in the 1910s under Sun Yat-sen's newly founded republic, foundered on the disillusionment with the Europeans that came with World War I and the subsequent lack of support from the West in resisting Japan's imperial ambitions in Asia. Those Chinese intellectuals of the "May Fourth" (1919) era who saw in socialism and the Russian revolution a way to modernize their country came to power in 1949, after long years of political rivalry and civil war with the more Western-oriented Nationalists. Yet even the Communists, after less than a decade of alliance with the Soviet Union, rejected the Stalinist model of development and, under Mao's insistent leadership, continued the country's search for its own road to restored national greatness.

Given this century of frustrating and inconstant efforts to modernize the country, it is remarkable that China's contemporary leaders have once again turned to the West for approaches to economic and social modernization. The leaders who shape China's policies today are perhaps wiser about the pitfalls of trying to bring what is still a peasant society into the twentieth century; yet they may prove to be no more successful than their predecessors in reconciling the dilemmas of the modernization process.

For American officials who negotiate with PRC counterparts, it is perhaps enough to be sensitive to the strong and conflicting emotions and the ambivalent perspectives that underlie Chinese dealings with the foreign world. On the one hand, the

2. See, for example, Deng-Kissinger, November 26, 1974.

Chinese seek the wealth and power of the industrialized West; on the other hand, they sustain a remarkable degree of self-confidence that they can modernize their country without losing China's own cultural and historical moorings. PRC officials stress (even as they send a new generation of intellectual talent to the United States for training in the sciences, engineering, and management) that they will construct their own brand of socialism, adapted to China's particular social and economic conditions.

The Chinese emphasize to foreigners the importance of being treated with "equality" and with full respect for their sovereignty and national independence. As Zhou Enlai told Henry Kissinger during their first meeting in July 1971, "The first question is that of equality, or in other words, the principle of reciprocity. All things must be done in a reciprocal manner."[3] But reciprocity does not necessarily mean adopting foreign ways; and the demand for equality conflicts with their own historical sense that China, by virtue of its size and past greatness, is more than just equal.

To resolve these ambivalent feelings about the West, the Chinese assert that they are just another mistreated and struggling developing country—even as they presume to the leadership of the Third World. And it is no accident that when China sought to reengage the rest of the world at the end of the Cultural Revolution, it did so by way of "ping-pong diplomacy," making political use of a sport in which the Chinese were world champions—and thus were "number one," even as Zhou, with artful tact, instructed his player/diplomats to stress "friendship first, competition second." Similarly, Mao stressed the slogan "never seek hegemony" as part of his country's defense policy; yet Zhou, in a candid moment, acknowledged to Kissinger the difficulties of keeping Chinese sentiments of "big-nation chauvinism" in check:

> *The objective fact of the largeness of the Chinese nation and Chinese area easily create a tendency to nationalistic sentiments and big nation chauvinism. [But] if there are too strong nationalist feelings, then one will cease to learn from others; one will seal oneself in and believe one is the best or will cease to learn from the strong points of others.*[4]

---

3. Zhou-Kissinger, July 9, 1971.

4. Zhou-Kissinger, February 18, 1973.

The overall effect of these complex feelings and conflicting attitudes is a hypersensitivity about being treated equally but with the special respect due a once and future great power; the inclination to discuss issues in a global context, even when China's national power lacks global reach; a self-righteous feeling that the world owes China special treatment for past injustices; and a tendency to side with the weak and oppressed, with whom the Chinese identify themselves, even as they assert China's status as a world leader.

Relationships: The Games of *Guanxi*

In contrast to the ambivalences of the Chinese about dealings with the outside world, they seem to manage the interpersonal aspects of the negotiating process with great self-assurance. To a remarkable degree, they are able to create their own "world" in structuring a negotiation with a foreign government. China's Confucian tradition places supreme value on the cultivation and management of interpersonal relations, *guanxi;* and in the negotiating process, contemporary Chinese seek to recreate their own social context and enmesh the foreign negotiator in a process that they can manage to their own advantage.

Chinese society is strongly collectivist and *inter*dependent. Individualism is eschewed as "selfishness." The mutual obligations that are an essential aspect of the Confucian tradition envelop the individual in a web of relationships that limit his personal initiative even as they give security to the larger social collective, be it family, village, or work unit. The foreign businessman, operating in this social context, finds that his Chinese counterparts seek to establish relations of "friendship" with him, but their expectations of friends far exceed American notions of that concept (see Pye, 1982, pp. 85–91).

The foreign negotiator, operating in a context where matters of authority, power, and sovereignty impart a hierarchical character to the negotiating process, finds that the Chinese have a remarkable capacity to maneuver him into the role of supplicant or *demandeur*—even in circumstances where the realities of the situation clearly put the Chinese in the position of having to ask something from the foreigner. Ambivalence about dealing with the foreign world and enduring Chinese fears about being taken advantage of by wily foreigners lead PRC political negotiators to adopt the more secure posture of being the superior rather than the dependent in a relationship.

Draw the Adversary in . . . to a Dependent Position

> Carter: *When I returned to Washington [from a trip to Illinois and West Virginia], Zbig [Brzezinski] had come back from China. He was overwhelmed with the Chinese. I told him he had been seduced. (Carter, 1982, p. 196)*

When the Chinese decide their interests are served by building a relationship with a foreign country, they can be highly skilled in drawing the officials of that country into personal relationships.[5] Many former U.S. officials with extensive experience in dealings with the Chinese recall that their early encounters with PRC officials did not really seem to be negotiations at all, but rather very general exchanges of view or social encounters in which the Chinese assessed the attitudes and motives of the American side in wanting to establish a relationship with the PRC. One former official observed that the boundaries of a negotiation with the Chinese are often hard to identify, because much of the activity in the preliminary stages—broad discussion of issues, sightseeing trips, and banquet talk—seems unrelated to concrete issues of concern. Yet it is evident, in retrospect, that the Chinese use such encounters as part of a purposeful process of establishing personal relationships.

This impulse to build relationships reflects a highly personalized view of the political process. In one of the early U.S.-PRC exchanges carried out indirectly via the intermediation of the Pakistan government, Zhou Enlai expressed concern that President Nixon's reference to his desire to establish "secret links" between the two countries meant only that he wanted to establish

---

5. This is in marked contrast to their behavior when they do *not* want to build a relationship—as was the case with the United States in the early 1950s. At Panmunjom, and at various times in the Geneva ambassadorial talks, the behavior of PRC diplomats was obviously calculated to keep the United States at arm's length, or at most to create a relationship of adversaries rather than friends. See Dean (1966), Johnson (1984), Joy (1955), and Young (1968).

a "hot line" communication channel such as the United States had with the Soviet Union.[6] In fact, Nixon intended to send a personal envoy secretly to China to prepare the way for his own visit; and Zhou Enlai later recalled with emphasis how important it had been to PRC leaders involved in initiating the normalization dialogue that Nixon was willing to deal with them at a personal level: "From the beginning he [Nixon] took the attitude he was willing to come to Beijing to meet us."[7]

Zhou's comment reflects the unspoken assumption that a foreign leader is best influenced when a personal relationship has been established, when his attitudes and motivations have been explored, and when enough of a commitment to the relationship has been created to make the foreigner vulnerable to the various forms of appeal and pressure that can be applied to "old friends." This fundamental instinct is different in kind, but not necessarily in effect, from Chinese notions of adversarial relationships. A basic Maoist military tenet of the Civil War era, as well as of more recent times, is that of "drawing the enemy in deep" *(youdi shenru)* into Chinese Communist party–controlled territory, where he can be enmeshed in a "people's war." It was such a perspective that led PRC officials to *want* their Nationalist adversaries to occupy the offshore islands of Quemoy and Matsu as a point of pressure and a link between the mainland and Taiwan. As Zhou told Nixon in 1972:

> *We . . . advised [Chiang Kai-shek] not to withdraw from Quemoy and Matsu. We advised him not to withdraw by firing artillery shells at them—that is, on odd days we would shell them, and on holidays we would not shell them. So they understood our intentions and didn't withdraw. No other means or messages were required; just this method of shelling they understood.*[8]

Why should the Nationalists, or any foreign government, want to sustain a relationship on this basis, when they can anticipate that they will be subject to various forms of manipulation or pressure? This is precisely the question the Chinese seek to answer

---

6. See Nixon's discussion with Pakistani President Yahya Kahn, October 25, 1970.

7. Zhou-Kissinger, July 9, 1971.

8. Zhou-Nixon, February 24, 1972.

for themselves in the early, relationship-building stage of a negotiation. There is nothing magical about the process; the Chinese just assume that foreign leaders or officials have their own political motives and/or personal interests in approaching China, and if the Chinese can identify these motives and interests, they will be in a better position to enmesh their counterparts in the games of *guanxi*.[9]

In this early stage of contact, the Chinese frequently turn to trusted third parties to provide background information on the leader or official they will be dealing with or to serve as intermediaries in initial communications. Such an indirect approach, of course, was notable in the establishment of high-level U.S.-PRC contacts in 1970 and 1971. Rumania and Pakistan served as intermediaries between the Nixon White House and the Mao-Zhou leadership in Beijing, not only providing the Chinese with intelligence about the intentions of the Nixon administration, but also giving *bona fides* on the initial contacts, a measure of assurance that the two sides did, in fact, share common political objectives and that there would be no embarrassment or hostile confrontation.[10]

Who Needs Whom?

Chinese society has a deeply rooted authoritarian tradition; and despite contemporary assertions to U.S. officials of their concern about being treated as equals, the Chinese, in fact, feel most comfortable in relationships where positions of superior and subordinate, leader and dependent, have been clearly established.

---

9. It should be noted that the Chinese are just as sensitive to identifying counterpart officials who will *not* be drawn into an "old friend" relationship. At least two recent American secretaries of state and one national security adviser were considered by the Chinese to be too aloof or uninterested in building a relationship or too hostile to serve the Chinese officials' purposes. While these individuals were in office, the Chinese proceeded to cultivate relationships with other Americans who they anticipated would be more receptive to their approaches, or who shared common policy perspectives or political objectives.

10. Zhou told Kissinger in their first encounter how important it had been that Pakistani President Yahya Khan had vouched for Nixon's seriousness of intent in wanting to normalize U.S.-PRC relations. And Zhou used Yahya to pass on to Nixon the sensitive message that if the United States made it appear that China was approaching out of weakness or fear of the Soviet Union, the normalization process would not go forward (Kissinger-Hilaly, February 26, 1970).

Thus a major aspect of the relationship game is a testing of who needs whom, assessing the motives and needs that lead a counterpart government or official to want to sustain a relationship within which specific issues will be resolved in favor of the interests of one party or the other (if not both).[11]

As noted earlier, China's experience with foreign powers over the past century leads PRC officials to want to avoid the subordinate position in a relationship.[12] It is politically devastating in the Chinese context for a leader to put the country in the position of appearing to be dependent on a foreign power. Thus, at the beginning of the normalization process, the Chinese reacted sharply when their first grain purchases from the United States were characterized by a U.S. Department of Agriculture spokesman as reflecting the PRC's inability to produce sufficient grain to meet domestic consumption requirements. To suggest that the government is unable to feed its own people and must rely on foreign sources of supply is to challenge the very legitimacy of political leadership in China.[13]

The "who needs whom" theme runs throughout the evolution of the U.S.-PRC relationship during the 1970s. At the conclusion

---

11. For a discussion of this theme in Soviet political culture, see Leites (1951), pp. 40–41.

12. It should be observed, of course, that the Chinese, in fact, *have* established relationships in which they voluntarily assumed a subordinate position, as with the West during the May Fourth period in the 1910s and most obviously in the relationship with the "elder brother" Soviet Union in the 1950s. The disappointments in these relationships, however, only reinforced Chinese instincts to be independent, or at least to be the predominant power in an international relationship, as they were with Albania, their sole, small ally during the 1960s.

By 1985, the Chinese had again opened the door to an intensive relationship with the outside world—particularly the United States and the other industrialized democracies. It is noteworthy that as China's leaders increased their interdependence with the outside world in the late 1970s, they began to stress a foreign-policy line of independence, as if verbal assertions of autonomy would counteract the fact of their growing interdependence with the world. Thus, the more *interdependent* the Chinese become, the more likely they are to seek the reassurance of at least verbal assertions of independence.

It is this tension between fears of being misused (again) by foreign powers and the country's objective need for trade, cultural, and even security relations with the outside world that imparts much of the tension and dynamic to China's contemporary foreign relations.

13. See Kissinger-Huang Hua, September 19, 1972; also Solomon-Ji Chaozhu, October 25, 1974.

of Kissinger's first, secret trip to Beijing, the one troublesome issue in drafting a communiqué was the Chinese effort to phrase the announcement so as to make it appear that President Nixon had asked to visit the PRC.[14] Similarly, in 1973, Zhou Enlai maneuvered the discussion about establishing liaison offices to make it evident that the United States had asked for them.[15] Having the foreigner come to them for something not only reinforces the legitimacy of the Chinese leaders and strengthens their own position, it also establishes a certain measure of psychological dominance in the relationship.

U.S.-PRC discussions of strategic issues have been suffused with the issue of which side is more in need of the relationship. Kissinger's exchanges with Zhou Enlai, Qiao Guanhua, and Deng Xiaoping during the 1970s are a continuous and unresolved exploration of the question of whether China or the United States is the primary target of Soviet hegemony. In response to a Nixon statement to Mao Zedong on February 21, 1972, that the Soviets had positioned more of their military forces against the PRC than against Europe,[16] Chinese leaders developed the slogan of the Soviets "feinting toward the East to attack in the West" (Zhou Enlai, 1973, p. B-8) as a way of reassuring their own people that they were not the primary target of Soviet pressures—and also to counter the assumed U.S. presumption that China needed a relationship with the West for security reasons. Thus, Kissinger's exchanges with his PRC interlocutors endlessly explored Chinese assertions that the primary Soviet strategic objective was Europe; that Soviet forces in Asia were targeted primarily on U.S. naval forces and regional bases; that the Soviets' "southern strategy" of intervention in the Middle East, Afghanistan, India, and Indochina was really part of the effort to outflank Europe and gain control of Western oil reserves and sea lanes of communication; and that China did not fear Soviet military pressures.

---

14. See Kissinger (1979), p. 751; also the Zhou-Kissinger exchanges of July 10–11, 1971.

15. The liaison offices were first proposed by the U.S. side in counterpart talks on October 21, 1971 (Xiung Xianghui-Holdridge, October 21, 1971).

16. In fact, the reverse is true. About one-quarter of the Soviet forces were deployed against the PRC, the remainder against Europe and the United States.

The unspoken message in these exchanges is the concern of Chinese leaders that if they appear to need the United States too much, they will once again be taken advantage of by a foreign power, especially regarding their objective of recovering Taiwan. This was most pungently phrased by Chairman Mao in an exchange with Kissinger in 1975:

> Mao: *We see that what you are doing is leaping to Moscow by way of our shoulders, and these shoulders are now useless. . . .*
>
> Kissinger: *We have nothing to gain in Moscow.*
>
> Mao: *But you can gain Taiwan in China.*
>
> Kissinger: *We can gain Taiwan in China?*
>
> Mao: *But you now have the Taiwan of China.*
>
> Kissinger: *But we will settle that between us.*
>
> Mao: *In a hundred years.*
>
> Kissinger: *That's what the Chairman said the last time I was here.*[17]

Similarly, in 1981 and 1982, the Chinese resisted the development of programs of strategic cooperation with the United States until they had established at least some limits on U.S. arms sales to Taiwan. This was an effort to turn the "who needs whom" game around on the United States, to make American leaders face the prospect of a breakdown in the relationship—or at least the prospect of no Chinese cooperation in strategic matters—until PRC demands regarding American arms sales to Taiwan had been met.

The Chinese realized full well that the United States was not about to assume a subordinate position relative to the PRC any more than the PRC was going to volunteer to be treated as a junior partner or "younger brother" of the United States—despite the needs of the two countries for a relationship. The rhetorical way out of this dilemma for the Chinese was to assert that they are independent and self-reliant, and that they seek no favors from the United States. As Deng Xiaoping said to Kissinger in the fall of 1975:

---

17. Mao-Kissinger, October 21, 1975.

We believe China should rely on its independent strength in dealing with the Soviets, and China has never asked for favors from others . . . frankly, China fears nothing under heaven or on earth. China will not ask favors from anyone. We depend on the digging of tunnels. We rely on millet plus rifles to deal with all problems internationally and locally, including the problems in the East. There is an argument in the world to the effect that China is afraid of an attack by the Russians. As a friend, I will be candid and tell you that this assessment is wrong.[18]

Such verbal bravado, of course, ran into the realities of China's defense and modernization needs, and its military and economic weaknesses relative to the Soviet Union. And at times the Chinese *did* ask for things from the United States, most notably technology. But PRC leaders will go to great lengths to avoid a situation in which they appear to be the supplicant. At most, they can acknowledge, as did Mao, that China and the United States need each other. As the Chairman rhetorically inquired of Kissinger in the fall of 1975:

Yesterday, in your quarrel with the Vice Prime Minister [Deng] you said the United States asked nothing of China, and China asked nothing of the United States. As I see it, this is partly right and partly wrong. . . . If neither side had anything to ask from the other, why would you be coming to Beijing? If neither side had anything to ask, then why did you want to come to Beijing, and why would we want to receive you and the President?[19]

There can be no easy resolution of the "who needs whom" issue with the Chinese, because their objective needs for an active relationship with the Western world are in tension with their presumptions to being an independent, global power and their fears of being taken advantage of in a dependent relationship with a more powerful foreign nation. At best, the issue can be defused as a source of pretense or pressure in negotiating encounters by neither humiliating the proud Chinese for their needs and vulnerabilities nor "kowtowing" to their desires to be treated as more than an equal or their exaggerated assertions of self-reliance and Third World leadership.

---

18. Deng-Kissinger, October 20, 1975.

19. Mao-Kissinger, October 21, 1975.

Your Relationship with China Is in Doubt: Show Us You Care

A variation of the "who needs whom" theme is the manipulation of foreign officials so as to cast doubt and uncertainty on their relationship with China. A high-level political figure who has established some reputation in his own country and in the international community for being skillful in dealing with the Chinese can be significantly threatened by having his status as a "friend of China" thrown in doubt. The official or negotiator is put in the position of having to "deliver" so that the Chinese will sustain his relationship with them, or face a loss of respect, prestige, and political influence. Such was the game the Chinese played with Kissinger in 1974–1975 when they wanted him to complete the normalization process, and with George Bush in 1980 and 1982 when they wanted assurances from the Reagan administration that it would not "turn back the clock" on U.S. China policy.[20]

Perhaps the clearest example of Chinese maneuvering to draw an administration into proving its interest in a relationship is the early dealings of the Carter administration with the PRC. During the 1976 presidential campaign and in the first months of his administration, President Carter and his senior officials gave uncertain signals about their interest in a relationship with the PRC and in completing the normalization process (Oksenberg, 1982). In the two years that followed, the Chinese turned this situation —in which *they* were the uncertain party about a U.S. administration's interest in a relationship with them—into one in which they had the administration going to some lengths to demonstrate its desire to develop a relationship with the PRC.

When Secretary of State Cyrus Vance went to Beijing in August 1977, the Chinese heard him out on international and bilateral issues, including a presentation of the administration's approach to normalization. But they held themselves aloof from him, rejecting his suggestion for a joint press communiqué to publicize the results of his trip and characterizing his visit both privately and publicly as a "step backward" in the relationship. The Chinese position reflected, in part, uncertainties in their own approach

---

20. These examples are explored in more detail below.

to dealing with the United States, but it also expressed PRC concerns about Vance as an official they could work with, given his views on the Soviet Union and on normalization and their desire to press the United States for more favorable terms for normalization.

The following spring, the administration decided it wanted to accelerate the pace of normalization, and National Security Adviser Zbigniew Brzezinski put himself forward to the Chinese as a friendly interlocutor in this process (Brzezinski, 1983, pp. 202–203). Brzezinski went to China in May 1978 with instructions to assure the Chinese that "the President has made up his mind" about normalization—a phrase PRC officials had been using with U.S. counterparts since the Vance visit to Beijing the preceding year. Brzezinski persistently tried to convince the Chinese that President Carter *was* serious about normalization, while the Chinese artfully cast doubts on his assertion in order to put him in the position of having to do more to prove himself:

> Brzezinski: *At the outset I would like to express to you our determination to move forward on the process of normalization. I can say on behalf of President Carter that the United States has made up its mind on this issue. . . .*
>
> *As I said when I began, the U.S. has made up its mind on this issue. I certainly am anxious to do anything I can to enhance and accelerate this process.*[21]
>
> . . . .
>
> Huang Hua: *On the Chinese side, we have raised three conditions on normalization of relations between our two countries. . . . China has done its utmost to accommodate the views of the U.S. . . . So the Chinese position cannot be changed. . . . Let no one harbor any hope that the Chinese side will make any concessions in this respect. If the U.S. side gives consideration to this point . . . and really makes up its mind, it is not difficult to solve this issue.*[22]
>
> . . . .
>
> Deng Xiaoping: *You must be tired [from your long trip].*
>
> Brzezinski: *I am exhilarated.*

21. Huang Hua-Brzezinski, May 20, 1978.

22. Huang Hua-Brzezinski, May 21, 1978.

. . . .

Deng: *The question now remains how to make up one's mind [on whether or not to normalize]. President Ford stated [in 1975] that if he were reelected he would move to full normalization according to the three conditions without any reservation. We were very happy at that time with the oral commitment of President Ford. . . . Subsequently President Ford was not reelected, and of course the new administration has a right to reconsider this question. . . .*

I think that is about all on this question. We are looking forward to the day when President Carter makes up his mind. Let's now shift the subject.

Brzezinski: *I have told you before, President Carter* has *made up his mind.*

Deng: *So much the better.*[23]

In addition to demonstrating how the Chinese can hold off an interlocutor to entice him to accommodate to their position, this series of exchanges emphasizes the Chinese concern with the counterpart official's *attitude* as a basis for building a relationship: The president should "make up his mind." Reflecting the concerns with "correct thinking" and thought reform that have been fundamental aspects of both the Confucian tradition and Chinese communism (Lifton, 1963), PRC negotiators place considerable emphasis on exploring the *attitudes* of their counterparts, their feelings and views about China, and their positions on international issues of concern to the PRC. The Chinese concluded that in Brzezinski they had an interlocutor with congruent views on the Soviet Union (which was not the case in their assessment of Secretary of State Vance) and an official who was willing to put himself forward in building a normal relationship with China, "to do anything I can to enhance and accelerate this process."[24]

23. Deng-Brzezinski, May 21, 1978.

24. Another example of Chinese concern with a counterpart official's attitude as the basis for building a relationship was Chinese uncertainty about the Reagan administration's position on China policy. In the early 1980s, Deng Xiaoping repeatedly expressed concern about U.S. technology-transfer policy, not only because of a desire to acquire advanced American technology, but also because of what the Reagan administration's policy on transfers revealed about its *attitude* toward the PRC. As Deng said to Secretary of the Treasury Donald Regan, "America has not given China a single item of advanced technology. . . . I wonder whether the United States is still not treating China as a hostile country." (Deng-Regan, November 19, 1981; see also Deng-Mondale, November 22, 1981)

The Chinese instinct to pressure foreign officials by casting doubt on their relationship with China was also illustrated by their use of the tactic of playing political adversaries against each other in their dealings with the Carter administration. The Chinese sought to use a presumed Vance-Brzezinski rivalry to their benefit (just as they put pressure on Henry Kissinger by playing up to Secretary of Defense James Schlesinger and by encouraging Secretary of State Alexander Haig against National Security Adviser Richard Allen).[25] In none of these instances did the Chinese do anything to create a rivalry—it was there for them to respond to or to ignore. But in each instance, they sought to advance their interests by making one official in the rivalry concerned about his relationship with China, or by drawing into the relationship the official they considered more friendly to their position.

PRC officials also use the millennial Chinese imperial tradition in controlling access to their senior leaders as a way to build the foreigner's uncertainty about his relationship with China, thus giving him an incentive to be forthcoming in meeting Chinese conditions. During his first trip to the PRC, Kissinger sparred with Zhou Enlai about whether or not President Nixon would have to agree to establish diplomatic relations with the PRC (and break relations with Taiwan) as a condition for meeting Chairman Mao:

> Zhou: *You mentioned that the meeting today is an historic occasion. Of course, a still greater historic occasion would be if President Nixon comes to China and meets Chairman Mao Zedong. That would be an historic occasion, if we could solve problems. . . .*
>
> *Therefore, the question of Taiwan becomes one regarding which we cannot but blame your government. . . . If this crucial question is not solved, then the whole question [of U.S.-PRC relations] will be difficult to solve. . . . When your President comes to discuss matters with Chairman Mao Zedong, the conclusion could be drawn that he will answer that question [about the timing of the establishment of diplomatic relations]. . . .*
>
> Kissinger: *Is the Prime Minister linking a meeting between the President and Chairman Mao Zedong to the prior establishment of diplomatic relations, or can the two be separated?*

---

25. This tactic is explored in more detail in Chapter Three.

> Zhou: *This is not absolute. Of course, it should be discussed. If time is needed, it may not necessarily be solved then. However, the general direction should be established.*[26]

As it turned out, Nixon did meet with Mao at the beginning of his visit to China, although the timing of the meeting was a surprise to the president (notification came just as Nixon was preparing to shower on the day of his arrival in Beijing). A second Mao-Nixon meeting, which Zhou had said would occur, never took place because—said the Chinese—the chairman had a cold. One may speculate, however, that Mao canceled what would have been an unprecedented second meeting with a foreign head of state on a single visit because he did not get all he wanted from Nixon on the Taiwan issue. The Chinese similarly held President Ford at arm's length to entice him to complete the normalization process.[27] Ford went to the PRC in December 1975 uncertain about arrangements for a meeting with Chairman Mao, only to have the visit occur as a surprise during a sightseeing tour of the Temple of Heaven.

In 1981, the Chinese first agreed to, then delayed, and finally postponed a visit to the United States by their director of Defense Research and Engineering, General Liu Huaqing.

The ultimate Chinese use of the relationship game is the threat to break off the relationship entirely—what one U.S. official has termed "the Chinese wife syndrome." In traditional Chinese society, wives, concubines, and other dependents of those in authority had few means to protect their interests beyond appeals to human sentiments, social convention, and public pressure. The most extreme pressure that such a dependent could bring to bear was to threaten suicide, which would bring the greatest loss of face to the offending authority and would leave him abandoned by depriving him of a loyal supporter. The Chinese have also used the threat of ending the relationship to pressure the United States.

---

26. Zhou-Kissinger, July 9, 1971.

27. They played Nixon against Ford by inviting the disgraced former president and other members of his family to China in late 1975 and early 1976, when it was politically embarrassing to Ford.

Thus, the establishment and manipulation of a relationship, even to the extreme of threatening to break it off when fundamental state interests are involved, is the central psychological theme in Chinese negotiating behavior.

The Bureaucratic Context

> Kissinger: *One of the most remarkable gifts of the Chinese is [the ability] to make the meticulously planned appear spontaneous. (Kissinger, 1979, p. 709)*

While the development and manipulation of personal relationships is a distinctive aspect of the Chinese approach to negotiations, official encounters with PRC negotiators take place in a more-or-less evident bureaucratic context. There is a certain irony in the contrast between the ties of friendship that Chinese officials seek to develop with their foreign counterparts and the strict bureaucratic and political discipline within which they operate. It is as if the Chinese view the constraints of organizational life as necessary to contain the very human qualities they seek to engage and manipulate in foreign officials.

Bureaucratic routine did not always encumber U.S. dealings with the PRC in the normalization period. The first American contacts with Beijing's officials in the early 1970s took place when the Chinese were just rebuilding their foreign relations after the Cultural Revolution—a domestic political frenzy that decimated the state bureaucracies. Much of the contact between Chinese and American officials between 1971 and 1976 took place under the direct personal management of Mao Zedong, Zhou Enlai, and their operatives in the Foreign Ministry.[28]

Since the completion of normalization in late 1976, however, the relationship has become increasingly bureaucratized, in part because of the formalization that came with establishment of

---

28. The "America managers" were a small and identifiable group: Just below Mao and Zhou at the senior political level was Marshal Ye Jianying; and in the Foreign Ministry were Vice Foreign Minister Qiao Guanhua, Huang Hua, Zhang Wenjin, Huang Zhen, Tang Wensheng ("Nancy Tang"), Wang Hairong, Han Xu, Ji Chaozhu, and the ever-present note-taker Lian Zhengbao. The composition of this group remained the same until Mao's death.

diplomatic relations and the signing of various treaties and agreements, but also because the Deng Xiaoping leadership purposefully rebuilt the state system, reconstituting much of the bureaucratic structure of state power that Mao destroyed in the Cultural Revolution. In the 1980s, the Sino-American relationship and U.S.-PRC negotiations, such as those leading to the August 17, 1982, communiqué on U.S. arms sales to Taiwan, were managed largely by the Foreign Ministry (with political oversight, to be sure, by senior leaders such as Deng Xiaoping and Zhao Ziyang).

Many of the issues that have been subjects of U.S.-PRC diplomatic exchanges or negotiation—including civil aviation, textiles and grain trade, and nuclear cooperation—involve the interests and the internal decisionmaking procedures of ministries and agencies under the State Council. As the context within which the Chinese negotiator operates has become bureaucratized and issues have become increasingly technical, the influence of senior political leaders has been somewhat diluted. Thus China's millennial bureaucratic tradition, along with the legacy of the Communist party's Marxist-Leninist organizational life, is finding renewed expression.

What are the primary qualities of the bureaucratic context within which PRC officials operate? Past experience suggests the characteristics described below.

Meticulous Planning and Management

As Henry Kissinger discovered during his first trip to Beijing, the Chinese pay meticulous attention to the organizational formalities of their dealings with foreign governments—but with an apparent ease that may deceive the foreign official regarding the degree of purpose and planning with which he is being dealt. The Chinese have traditionally considered form and ritual to be as important as substance in political and social relationships; indeed, form and ritual are not considered to be separate from substance.[29] This attitude is evident in their meticulous

Form and Ritual

29. For discussion of this point, see Yu (1968) and Fried (1969).

attention to protocol. Numerous examples could be cited, particularly in their preparations for the U.S. presidential visits they have hosted. A clear and brief statement of their concern with matters of form appears in a 1980 discussion about a proposed visit to the United States of then–Secretary General of the Party's Military Affairs Commission Geng Biao, at the invitation of the U.S. Secretary of Defense. As the director of the Defense Ministry's Foreign Affairs Bureau said to his American interlocutor:

> *Your Secretary of Defense [Harold Brown] invited Geng Biao face-to-face yesterday during their meeting to visit the United States. Geng did not respond. I have not had time to ask him about it yet. I will seek his instructions. As we see it, his military post as Secretary-General of the Military Commission is a Party post. Perhaps you have noted that in our press we only use his governmental post, Vice Premier, not his Party post.*[30]

The Chinese eventually resolved their protocol problem by appointing Geng to the state post of Minister of Defense, a role in which he traveled to the United States in May 1980.

Despite their relatively unmodernized communication system, the Chinese have shown a remarkable capacity to orchestrate all aspects of official encounters with foreign governments: the coordination of multiple channels of contact; the meshing of negotiating sessions with their internal decisionmaking procedures; use of sightseeing trips and banquets to pace a negotiation; use of the Chinese press and nongovernmental "friends" as adjunct "voices" in sending signals to the counterpart government during a negotiation, etc.

In pacing negotiations, the Chinese have also demonstrated a great sensitivity to the interplay between political processes in their own country and those in the counterpart government. During Kissinger's first encounter with Zhou, the premier revealed that he had already anticipated the time-phasing of the normalization negotiations:

> Zhou: *There are two questions I would like to clarify. I see the necessity for a period of time [to accomplish normalization], but the*

30. McGiffert-Chai Chengwen, January 8, 1980.

time that is left for President Nixon is limited. And as a close associate of his, you must be quite clear about this point.

Kissinger: *What is the Prime Minister's estimate of the time left to President Nixon?*

Zhou: *I see two stages. The first is one-and-a-half years; and the second, if he is reelected, five-and-a-half years. This would take us to the 200th anniversary of your country.*

Kissinger: *Which time period is the Prime Minister talking about, five-and-a-half years or one-and-a-half years?*

Zhou: *When your President comes . . . the conclusion could be drawn that . . . he will answer that question.*[31]

Similarly, the Chinese have shown considerable understanding of the way congressional procedures, politically significant anniversary dates, and official visits to and from the United States can be used as occasions for moving a negotiation along or putting pressure on the counterpart government to conclude an agreement.

Effective Briefing

PRC officials are usually well briefed on all aspects of a negotiating encounter. From the very first meetings between Zhou and Kissinger, it was evident that the Chinese had done considerable background research on each of the individuals in Kissinger's entourage, for the premier would use the occasion of the first, informal session of a visit to make some personal observation about each of them:

After a group picture was taken at the entrance to the meeting room, Zhou [Enlai] seated us behind the inevitable cups of green tea and proceeded to say a few words of personal greeting to everyone in the party. The Premier had done his biographical homework well and flattered my associates with references to their educational or professional history. . . . (Kissinger, 1979, p. 777)

Similarly, Zhou indicated that he had read Nixon's *Six Crises,* had seen the President's favorite movie ("Patton"), and was being kept up to date on U.S. press materials relevant to the development of the U.S.-China relationship. He had even seen

31. Zhou-Kissinger, July 9, 1971.

the reports of a speech given by President Nixon at Kansas City on July 6, 1971, which Kissinger himself had not seen because of his travels.

Much of the information the Chinese obtain about their foreign counterparts seems based on a careful reading of the press and the keeping of meticulous records of past encounters, rather than covert intelligence collection. Mao Zedong once ridiculed intelligence reporting and revealed that during the Cultural Revolution he had seen the first signals of a shift in Nixon's China policy by reading a 1967 article by Nixon in *Foreign Affairs* and then following subsequent newspaper accounts of policy reassessments in the Department of State.

The important point for the American negotiator is that the Chinese have shown a sophisticated capacity to assemble and orchestrate the use of information derived from multiple sources, such as the world's mass media and technical documentation, in support of negotiations and other official dealings with foreign governments, despite significant limitations in China's organizational outreach and technological capabilities.

Political Discipline

The Chinese negotiator operates with a political discipline reflecting the Leninist tradition of the Chinese Communist party—to which he almost certainly belongs. American negotiators with considerable experience in dealing with PRC counterparts remark that they often can "feel" the presence in the room of unseen audiences to whom their Chinese interlocutors are speaking: superiors whom the PRC officials must impress with their loyalty and toughness in implementing instructions; political rivals who will use any lapses in performance against them; and even foreign allies who are worrying that China may compromise their interests.

During Kissinger's secret trip to Beijing in 1971, Zhou proposed at the conclusion of their discussions that they tape-record a summary of their views. While the tape recording was never made—Kissinger resisted the suggestion—it does emphasize the multiple audiences, many of them unseen, who are "present" on the Chinese side of a negotiating table.

PRC officials demonstrate a remarkable capacity to hew to the party line on almost any issue of significance, and the consistency with which different officials invoke the same phrasing on a given matter reflects what must be written instructions or briefs that they follow closely. Particularly on matters relating to domestic politics, the Chinese present a united front to foreign officials, even when signs of leadership disarray are evident to the non-Chinese reader of the official press. A leader as senior as Zhou Enlai apparently could tell Henry Kissinger about the Cultural Revolution only with some trepidation—and perhaps at the instruction of Chairman Mao:

> *So I told you of our [Cultural Revolution] transformation during lunch. We do not cover up the facts of our transformation. When your President comes and talks to Chairman Mao he will speak much more. We sometimes wonder whether we can talk about such things. But Chairman Mao speaks completely at his will.*[32]

As a general rule, only the top man, the senior political leader (when he is in an unchallenged position), is free to speak his mind to foreign observers and officials. Those in subordinate positions—even officials as senior as the premier, ministers, and vice chairmen—speak with restraint and a common voice bespeaking the discipline of "democratic centralism."

This tradition of political and bureaucratic discipline imparts some interesting patterns to the negotiating process. PRC officials will go to great lengths to draw out a foreign counterpart regarding his government's position on issues under negotiation. Corresponding efforts to draw out the Chinese in the initial stages of a negotiation, however, will elicit either banalities, "principled" abstractions, or strong assertions that the foreign official should present his position first. Only after the Chinese believe they understand the foreign government's position will they respond —and then only after the senior leader or the collective leadership has reviewed the first exchanges and formulated a reply. Thus, in Kissinger's early exchanges with Zhou, the premier politely heard him out, and then, after consulting with Chairman Mao and perhaps other senior leaders, sharply attacked

32. Zhou-Kissinger, July 10, 1971.

the U.S. position with a forceful presentation of the PRC point of view (Kissinger, 1979, p. 750).

Even very high level Chinese negotiators, such as the foreign minister, will display almost no flexibility in position until very late in what may have been months of exchanges—when it is believed that all the "give" in the adversary's position has been tested. Then, after collective review, the negotiator may present a compromise position. More likely, according to past experience, he will let the negotiation deadlock, and the senior leader will subsequently intervene to cut the knot of the impasse. In the Chinese system, political authority and discipline are both highly centralized and personalized in the position of the senior leader.

There are, of course, times when the senior political leader is weak (as was Hua Guofeng in 1976–1977, after he had become Mao's successor, or Deng Xiaoping just after his third rehabilitation in 1977–1978). In such circumstances, political direction is less sure, since there is no voice of ultimate authority, and the PRC negotiator will be tentative in pushing issues to resolution. He may stall or protract a negotiation with rigid and self-righteous assertions that China's principled policy—however abstractly defined—is the only possible position. He will hold to a defensive discipline even as negotiating exchanges become mired in repetition and uncertainty.

Immobilism can also occur when the ministries whose interests are engaged in a negotiation cannot reach a common position, when the political center is having trouble gaining the compliance of local authorities, or when a senior leader or leadership collective has not resolved its differences and established a common position. Yet even in such circumstances, the PRC negotiator will display remarkable discipline, refusing to disclose to his foreign counterpart the internal differences that are obstructing the creation of a unified Chinese bargaining position.

The Obscurity of China's Internal Politics

Kissinger: *What is the news from our friends in Beijing?*

Huang Zhen: *Some of you read our newspapers in Beijing, our broadcasts. Your colleagues must know [what the news is].*

Kissinger: *You have no secrets? You must be following our practice (laughter).*

Huang Zhen: *What needs to be broadcast will be broadcast. What needs to be published will be published.*

Kissinger: *So you have nothing to add?*

Huang Zhen: *According to Dr. Kissinger's usual arrangement, I will be pleased to listen to your views.*[33]

The political discipline observed by PRC officials is, in part, a reflection of unstated fears of the destructive effects on the Chinese political system of factional political rivalries—of which the Cultural Revolution power struggle is only the most recent and a particularly costly example. More than one PRC official has observed off the record that factional conflict within the leadership is a greater threat to the security of the country than is a prospective enemy invasion. (Indeed, a foreign invasion is viewed by the Chinese as a *unifying* political force, as was the Japanese invasion in the 1930s.)

What is interesting to an American observer of the Chinese political scene is the determined effort of PRC officials to deny the existence of rivalries within the top leadership and to obscure policy conflicts from foreign view. The strength of this attitude is only additional proof, if any were needed, that factional struggles are an inherent and disruptive aspect of the Chinese political order —as they are of *all* political systems. The need to present an image of leadership unity reflects a certain vulnerability, which is perhaps reinforced in the minds of PRC officials by the degree to which *they* try to use leadership rivalries they perceive in foreign governments for their own ends.

The fact is that factional conflicts *do* affect PRC policies relevant to the interests of other countries, and they influence PRC negotiating positions. In the case of U.S.-PRC relations, policy differences in the Chinese leadership that culminated in the Lin Biao episode of 1971—in which the PRC defense minister, Mao Zedong's designated successor, apparently tried to assassinate

33. Kissinger-Huang Zhen, July 7, 1975.

Mao and, when discovered, fled by plane toward the Soviet Union, only to die when his plane crashed in Mongolia—seem to have delayed the initiation of the normalization dialogue. Vice Foreign Minister Qiao Guanhua, in a retrospective discussion with Kissinger of efforts by the two governments to establish direct contact in the late 1960s, cryptically commented that efforts by the U.S. government to make contact with the PRC via the intermediation of the Dutch ambassador to Beijing had been blocked because of unfavorable "circumstances," by which he probably meant internal political problems:

> Kissinger: *We sent a message to you in 1969 through the Dutch ambassador in Beijing. Did you take our message seriously? Did you get it?*
>
> Qiao: *We did give serious consideration to it, but circumstances were not right.*
>
> Kissinger: *I don't think he was a good channel of communication to you.*
>
> Qiao: *No, it was not that. We did give consideration to it, but our circumstances were not right.*[34]

Mao was somewhat more forthright about the Lin Biao affair in his 1972 meeting with President Nixon: "In our country . . . there is a reactionary group which is opposed to our contact with you. The result was that they got on an airplane and fled abroad."[35] Mao went on to praise the U.S. government's ability to interpret such events,[36] but the relationship between Lin Biao's opposition to Mao and the chairman's establishment of direct contact with the Nixon administration remains obscure.[37]

There is circumstantial evidence that political attacks on Zhou Enlai in 1974, in the context of the "anti–Lin Biao, anti–Confucius" campaign, led the PRC to withdraw its proffered solution to the

34. Kissinger-Qiao, October 3, 1973.

35. Mao-Nixon, February 21, 1972.

36. According to Mao, "Throughout the whole world, the U.S. intelligence reports [on the Lin Biao incident] are comparatively accurate. The next was Japan. As for the Soviet Union, they finally went to dig out the corpses, but they didn't say anything about it" (Mao-Nixon, February 21, 1972).

37. For varying interpretations of the Mao-Lin rivalry, see Brown (1976) and Chang (1976).

private-claims/blocked-assets problem put forward the year before by the premier.[38] Similarly, it seems likely that PRC demands in the fall of 1973 that the United States remove the Marine Guard security contingent from its Beijing liaison office reflected rising influence in the leadership of the radical group centered around Mao's wife Jiang Qing—the faction later termed the Gang of Four —as they attacked Zhou and resisted the rehabilitation of Deng Xiaoping.[39]

It can also be inferred that differences within the leadership following the purge of the Gang of Four in October 1976 led the newly rehabilitated Deng to stall the initiation of concrete negotiations about normalization—a process Deng was able to bring to a successful conclusion eighteen months later, in the late fall of 1978, when his political position was much stronger (Oksenberg, 1982, p. 183).

The point of these domestic PRC political events is not just that they had a significant influence on the evolution of the Sino-American relationship—it is assumed that internal politics influence foreign relations for all countries—but that the Chinese go to such great lengths to deny the existence of leadership difficulties that are obviously occurring. During the period in the early 1970s when signs of leadership conflict were increasing in PRC media, the government took *active* steps to deny to U.S. officials the rumors of conflict between Zhou Enlai and Jiang Qing. In late 1971, a Chinese-American scientist (who had been received by Mao and Zhou) was sent by PRC leaders to approach NSC officials and assert, among other things, that rumors of conflict between Zhou and Jiang Qing were untrue. Foreign Ministry officials would strenuously assert during the "anti-Confucius" campaign of 1974 that the leadership was fully unified. And Liaison Office Chief Huang Zhen—who in the summer of 1975, when the Gang of Four was particularly rampant, brushed aside inquiries about conflict in the leadership (see the quote at the beginning of this section)—blithely asserted to Kissinger not long after the Gang

38. See the PRC message to the U.S. government of June 14, 1974.

39. See Lin Ping-Bruce, September 26, 1973.

had been purged that the political situation in his country "is now excellent."[40]

It is obviously important for the American negotiator to have as clear an assessment as possible of the state of the PRC leadership, for the strength of the top leader or the degree of conflict over policies and positions will have a significant influence on negotiating instructions and on the ability of the leadership to conclude and implement agreements.

How is the foreign observer to penetrate the ritualistic assertions of his PRC counterparts that the political situation in their country is "excellent," or at least to evaluate their tendency to downplay the significance of leadership conflicts? One must place considerable reliance on professional analysts of the PRC political scene and their practice of the all-too-arcane art of "Beijingology"—a derivative of the even more hoary science of Kremlinology, the interpretation of signs of conflict in the equally secrecy-conscious Soviet leadership.

In various negotiating encounters, senior PRC leaders have provided tantalizing hints to their American interlocutors about domestic political conflicts. Hence, it can be useful to comb the record of official negotiating exchanges for indicators of the condition of the leadership. As an example, in July 1971, Zhou hinted obliquely to Kissinger about Lin Biao's opposition to the establishment of U.S.-PRC contacts:

> *I would also like to take the opportunity to say we express thanks for the gifts which the President and you have sent to Chairman Mao, Lin Biao, and myself. You may say that Chairman Mao and I both send our regards to President Nixon. . . .*[41]

After Lin's death, the Chinese—not surprisingly—gave no explanation to the U.S. government about the events that had led to the grounding of the entire People's Liberation Army air force for more than a month. Indeed, Kissinger met with Huang Zhen in Paris (where Huang was then PRC ambassador) on September 13—the day after Lin's plane had crashed in Mongolia—and

40. Kissinger-Huang Zhen, December 21, 1976.

41. Zhou-Kissinger, July 11, 1971.

informed Kissinger that his second trip to Beijing could be scheduled in October. PRC officials did take the unusual step of reconfirming the visit in a separate message on October 3, 1971, presumably as an oblique way of saying that despite the (as yet unrevealed) leadership feud that had just played itself out *mu hou* ("behind the curtain," as the Chinese like to characterize such conflicts), the Mao-Zhou leadership was still in control and its invitation to President Nixon still stood.

A bit more than a month after the event, Zhou still only hinted obliquely to Kissinger about the Lin affair, quoting Mao's own premonition of the defense minister's betrayal: "Chairman Mao has a thesis: those who hail you are not the ones who support you. He said this to [author of *Red Star over China*] Edgar Snow [in December 1970]."[42] Ultimately it was Mao himself who had sufficient authority to reveal the event to President Nixon.

Mao also hinted at the growing troubles with Jiang Qing in the following February 1973 exchange with Kissinger:

> Mao: *The trade between our two countries at present is very pitiful. It is gradually increasing. You know China is a very poor country. We don't have much. What we have in excess is women (laughter).*
>
> Kissinger: *There are no quotas for those, or tariffs?*
>
> Mao: *So if you want them, we can give a few of those to you, some tens of thousands (laughter).*
>
> Zhou: *Of course on a voluntary basis.*
>
> Mao: *Let them go to your place. They will create disasters. That way you can lessen our burdens (laughter).*
>
> . . . .
>
> Mao: *Do you want our Chinese women? We can give you ten million (laughter).*
>
> Kissinger: *The Chairman is improving his offer.*
>
> Mao: *By doing so we can let them flood your country with disaster and therefore impair your interests. In our country we have too many women, and they have a way of doing things. They give birth to children and our children are too many (laughter).*

---

42. Zhou-Kissinger, October 21, 1971.

> Kissinger: *It is such a novel proposition, we will have to study it.*
>
> Mao: *We have so many women in our country that don't know how to fight.*
>
> Nancy Tang: *Not necessarily. There are women's detachments.*
>
> Mao: *They are only on stage. In reality if there is a fight you would flee very quickly and run into underground shelters.*
>
> . . . .
>
> Mao: *You know, the Chinese have a scheme to harm the United States, that is, to send ten million women to the United States and impair its interests by increasing its population.*
>
> Kissinger: *The Chairman has fixed the idea so much in my mind that I'll certainly use it in my next press conference (laughter).*[43]

Was Mao's humorous and condescending banter about women —their capacity to cause disasters, and their theatrical bravery— really a putdown of Jiang Qing? Given the Chairman's frequently cryptic dialogue, one cannot be certain. And even if his oblique deprecation of women was directed toward his wife, was he signaling his opposition to Jiang Qing or only misguiding Kissinger about the degree of support he in fact was giving to the woman who had been partly responsible for bringing the disaster of the Cultural Revolution down on China? The obscurity of Chinese politics persists, even when the top man chooses to comment on his domestic problems to a foreign official.

---

43. Mao-Kissinger, February 17–18, 1973.

Mao's wife was convincing him terrible ideas but as "mao's wife" people listened – in gang of 4

Very indirect – LISTEN understand interperate

3

The Process

Intergovernmental bargaining with the Chinese to solve specific problems or attain concrete goals, often expressed in published agreements, takes place within the context of the culture, history, and institutions explored in Chapter Two. We shall now assess the *process* of formal negotiation with the Chinese as the U.S. government has experienced it since 1970. This chapter describes evident patterns of style and action by which Chinese officials attempt to manage the negotiating process in the service of attaining agreements that will serve the interests of the PRC as they are defined by its senior leaders.

U.S. officials who have had considerable experience in dealing with the Chinese describe the negotiating process as a linear progression of rather well-defined and sequential stages (see Table 1): The first stage is a period of *opening moves,* in which the Chinese try to identify and establish a relationship with a favorable interlocutor, gain his or her commitment to certain "principles" they put forward, and establish a negotiating agenda favorable to Chinese objectives. What follows is often a lengthy *period of assessment,* in which the Chinese use a variety of facilitating

Table 1. The Linear Process of PRC Political Negotiations

(1) → **Opening Moves**	(2) → **Period of Assessment**	(3) → **End Game**	(4) → **Implementation**
• Establish a relationship with a "friendly" counterpart official • Establish a favorable agenda • Gain commitment to PRC "principles"	• Draw out interlocutor • Apply pressures • Test intentions, patience	• Conclude an agreement, or • Reserve position, or • Abort the negotiation	• Press for adherence • Make additional demands

maneuvers to draw out the foreign official on his or her government's position, objectives, and degree of flexibility. They may resort to a variety of pressure tactics—invoking past commitments to principles, the use of the media and public opinion, and time deadlines—to test the firmness of commitment of the counterpart government to its stand and to try to move it to accept the PRC's position. When the Chinese negotiators have concluded that there is no further "give" in their counterparts' position, and when PRC interests are served, they will swiftly initiate an *end game* or concluding phase in order to reach formal agreement. Attainment of a formal agreement is followed by a period of *implementation* in which the Chinese press for scrupulous adherence to the agreement reached and sometimes even make additional demands on the counterpart government.

We describe this process in greater detail below, using examples from U.S. experience in negotiating the Shanghai Communiqué of 1972, the U.S.-PRC normalization agreement of 1978, and the August 17, 1982, Joint Communiqué on U.S. arms sales to Taiwan.

Opening Moves

One former U.S. official interviewed for this study remarked that the boundaries of a negotiation with the Chinese are often hard to perceive, for a broad range of encounters and communications in the early phases of contact are, in the Chinese view, relevant to the construction of a relationship that will be drawn upon in the more formal periods of explicit bargaining.

Identify and Cultivate the Right Interlocutor

In hindsight, it is evident that PRC officials have carefully assessed a range of American officials in each of the U.S. administrations since the late 1960s and have purposefully encouraged those whose views they believed to be helpful to their own objectives and who appeared likely to be "friendly," to establish them as interlocutors in the normalization process. The criteria they have used in these assessments appear to have been a broad strategic and political outlook based on distrust of the Soviet Union, a consequent belief in the value to the United States of a normal relationship with the PRC, and easy access to the president (if the candidate was not the president himself).

The clearest example of such scouting is the case of Henry Kissinger. In early 1971, when the Chinese had decided to establish direct contact with the Nixon administration, PRC officials let it be known through at least two intermediaries that they were interested in meeting—not with an official of the Department of State, but with Kissinger, President Nixon's national security adviser. Vice Foreign Minister Qiao Guanhua made this point to the Norwegian ambassador in early February, and Pakistan's ambassador to Washington, Agha Hilaly, transmitted a similar message from Zhou Enlai on April 27, 1971. Even Chairman Mao, in his meeting with President Nixon on February 21, 1972, kept trying to bring Kissinger into the conversation, to Kissinger's embarrassment in his relationship with the president:

> Mao: *We two [Mao and Nixon] must not monopolize the whole show. It won't do if we don't let Dr. Kissinger have a say. You [Kissinger] have been famous about your trips to China.*

> Kissinger: *It was the President who set the direction and worked out the plan.*
>
> Nixon: *He is a very wise assistant to say it that way (Mao and Zhou laugh).*[1]

As noted earlier, President Carter's national security adviser, Zbigniew Brzezinski, put himself forward as a friendly interlocutor in late 1977, and the Chinese were quite prepared to go along with him, given his view of the Soviets, his relationship with the president, and their uncertainties about Secretary of State Cyrus Vance.

The Chinese were quite assertive during the first year of the Reagan administration in trying to establish Secretary of State Alexander Haig as the primary channel of communication. They were uncertain about where the president stood on China policy, and they had doubts about whether his national security adviser, Richard Allen, was prepared to be "friendly," so senior PRC officials pressed for an early visit to Beijing by Haig, whom they knew from the Nixon period and considered to be sympathetic.

It also appears that the Chinese concluded after Secretary of State George Shultz's visit to Beijing in February 1983 that Shultz was not inclined to be an active promoter of the U.S.-PRC relationship within the administration. Thus, because they did not wish the relationship to languish, they first tried to draw out Secretary of Defense Caspar Weinberger, and later the president himself.

In at least one instance, the PRC actively attempted to block the appointment of an individual they considered to be hostile to them. During the 1980 campaign, Chinese leaders met with their "old friend" George Bush, who had been dispatched to Beijing by presidential candidate Reagan to explain his position on China policy and to defuse growing tensions in the relationship. In a long and tense discussion on August 22, 1980, Deng Xiaoping skeptically asked Bush who Ray Cline was and whether Cline's views on China reflected Regan-Bush policy. Shortly after the election, Cline—who had put himself forward to PRC embassy personnel in Washington as the channel to the new administration —made a trip to Asia, during which he held a press conference

---

1. Mao-Nixon, February 21, 1972.

in Singapore at which he characterized the PRC as "uncivilized."[2] The Chinese, in an effort to embarrass Cline, whom they feared would be appointed Assistant Secretary of State for East Asian and Pacific Affairs in the new administration, published his remarks and attacked them vigorously to clearly indicate that he was unacceptable to them as a manager of U.S. China policy.[3]

It is natural enough that the Chinese, like any other government, want to see friendly officials in high places in a U.S. administration. What is notable in the Chinese case is the demonstrated effectiveness of the Chinese (Nationalist as well as PRC officials) in cultivating friendly advocates in administrations going back to the 1930s and the substantial expectations they have about the appropriate demands that can be made on "old friends." As discussed later in this chapter, the Chinese expect considerably more of their friends than accords with American notions of friendship; and when they want to bring pressure to bear on an administration they do it through their (hapless) friends.

Controlling the Ambience

> Kissinger: *After a dinner of Peking duck I'll agree to anything. (quoted in Qiao-Kissinger, February 24, 1972)*

The Chinese invariably seek to conduct negotiations on their home territory. The reasons for this are not difficult to assess; what is remarkable is their ability to manage relationships in a manner that inclines foreign powers from whom they seek political and economic benefits to concede this marginal but significant advantage.

Conducting negotiations in Beijing gives Chinese officials the greatest access to their technologically underdeveloped communications system and their internal decisionmaking procedures; but more important, it gives them a subtle psychological edge over their counterparts, who are somewhat disoriented—and most likely jet-lagged—in an unfamiliar physical environment. As with countless generations of foreigners who traveled with

2. See the *Los Angeles Times,* December 2, 1980, and *The New York Times,* December 2, 1980.

3. See Peng Di (1980), p. B-1, and Lu Yuan (1980).

great anticipation to the Middle Kingdom, meeting with present-day officials in China accords the Chinese leaders a measure of legitimacy and status that their real power may not warrant.

Apart from these considerations, negotiating in the Chinese capital gives the Chinese the opportunity to manage the ambience so as to maximize the sense of gratitude, dependence, awe, and helplessness they evoke in their guests. There is no little irony in the fact that the Chinese Communists, who seek to transform their peasant society into a modern, industrialized nation, use the trappings of imperial China—the palaces of the Forbidden City, the Ming Tombs, the Great Wall, and the cuisine and culture of a tradition they seek to outgrow—to impress foreign officials with their grandeur and seriousness of purpose.

There should be no doubt that the Chinese view the various forms of hospitality as part of the process of managing relations with foreigners. Internal documents of the Qing dynasty describe how the nineteenth-century mandarins sought to control the Europeans who intruded into the Middle Kingdom through the management of hospitality and information. As Manchu official Ch'i-ying described in an 1844 memorandum to the Emperor:

> *Sometimes we expose everything so that they will not be suspicious, whereupon we can dissipate their rebellious restlessness. Sometimes we have given them receptions and entertainment, after which they have had a feeling of appreciation. . . . The barbarians are born and grow up outside the frontiers of China, so that there are many things in the institutional system of the Celestial Dynasty with which they are not fully acquainted. . . . We must give them some sort of entertainment and cordial reception; but we are on guard against an intimate relationship in intercourse with them. (Fairbank and Teng, 1954, pp. 38–39)*

Kissinger's early impressions of PRC planning for the Nixon presidential visit convey a similar sense of the purposeful orchestration of receptions, sightseeing, cuisine, and music to dazzle a new generation of guests from afar. Kissinger noted that during his first two preparatory trips to Beijing—in which he was taken to the Forbidden City and the Great Wall and was shown contemporary Peking Opera—he had "been used by the meticulous Chinese as a guinea pig for their study of timings and required security precautions, as well as of how these strange Americans behaved in the presence of the wonders of Chinese history" (Kissinger, 1979, p. 1067). Banquets alternated with negotiating sessions in a way that controlled the level of tension as the difficult issues in a relationship strained by two decades of confrontation were explored by the two leaderships. Yet for all the gracious hospitality, Kissinger found himself negotiating the Shanghai Communiqué late at night after a banquet of Peking duck and powerful *mao tai* liquor. As he concluded, "nothing was accidental and yet everything appeared spontaneous" (Kissinger, 1979, p. 1056).

Lest the Chinese appear superhuman in their organizational skills, it should also be recorded that their efforts to control the ambience of a negotiation, while notable for meticulousness and apparent ease of effort, are not without an occasional gaffe. During the Nixon visit, the Chinese staged a casual "performance" by colorfully dressed youngsters equipped with toys and games at the Ming Tombs, one of the televised stops on the president's sightseeing tour. After the official party had left the scene, PRC officials collected the toys from the children—in sight of U.S. journalists who were in the process of packing up their equipment. This led one American correspondent to later question Zhou Enlai about the staged event—to which the premier replied self-critically that it had been wrong to have "put up a false appearance" (Kissinger, 1979, p. 1081).

During the Ford presidential visit in 1975, the Chinese had done their usual research on the president's favorite music, but they identified the president's alma mater incorrectly and played the Michigan State fight song rather than the University of Michigan's "Hail to the Victors." And during the visit of Vice President Walter Mondale in 1979, the Chinese delighted their guest by playing his favorite songs from "The Sound of Music" but left him most impressed with the degree of manipulation they were prepared to resort to in order to make a positive impression.

Any official who journeys to China more than two or three times will find his or her reactions to this purposeful management of the ambience changing from awe and apprehension to unease at such all-encompassing, set-piece hospitality. Even more discomfiting is the Chinese use of hospitality and protocol to build pressures on a visiting delegation. Precisely because the Chinese can be such superb hosts and have obviously gone to great lengths to make their foreign guests comfortable, it is all the more unsettling when they choose to use hospitality and protocol to insult.

In late 1975, the Chinese wanted to put maximum pressure on Kissinger and President Ford to complete the normalization process. Kissinger, on the first day of talks during his October advance trip to Beijing, indicated that he wanted to complete most of the negotiation of a joint communiqué before departing the capital, and to facilitate the process, he tabled a draft document at the end of the first session. The Chinese, to indicate their displeasure at the lack of movement toward full normalization, resorted to punctilious and excessive hospitality to stall the negotiation, even taking Kissinger and his party on an afternoon picnic in the Western hills to view the fall foliage—all as time to negotiate the joint document slipped away. Kissinger's increasingly insistent inquiries about the fate of the draft communiqué were blandly deflected with assurances that it was being translated. Finally, at midnight on the eve of Kissinger's departure, Foreign Minister Qiao Guanhua convened a post-banquet session to denounce the draft document and asserted that if there was to be any joint communiqué it had to be on Chinese terms—which, as conveyed to Kissinger during the late night session, were unacceptable to the U.S. side.

During the Ford visit a few months later, the Chinese did not use direct forms of insult to pressure the president, but they communicated their willingness to upstage him by inviting the disgraced Nixon—who was a domestic political embarrassment to Ford as the 1976 elections approached—and members of his family to China, and by keeping Ford in the dark as to whether and when he would meet with Chairman Mao.

In recent years, Americans have been spared the most offensive forms of Chinese adversarial negotiating practice, but it is worth recalling the kinds of circumstances in which the Chinese have used calculated insults and coldness to break down a negotiation, rather than hospitality to build a relationship. Arthur Dean, who negotiated with Huang Hua and Pu Shouchang at Panmunjom in 1953, recalled the lack of personal contact with a Chinese negotiating team that was determined to *prevent* reaching an agreement with the American side:

> *No individual could speak personally to anyone on the other side. There could be no exchanges even of ordinary amenities at the start or end of a meeting; the Chinese stared ahead, frozen-faced, ignoring our presence. It was forbidden to ask them, or the North Koreans, over to the U.N. side for a drink, a meal, or a conversation. . . . There was no way in which the normal tensions of difficult diplomatic negotiations could be relieved, and no way in which private negotiations or suggestions could be carried out. (Dean, 1966)*

In similar fashion, the Chinese resorted to calculated harassment and a range of insulting behaviors in 1949 to break the tattered remains of the U.S.-China relationship at the end of the Nationalist era (Johnson, 1984).

Establish a Favorable Agenda

During the 1950s and 1960s, the U.S. experience in adversarial negotiating encounters with the PRC was of a Soviet-style "battle of the agenda" (Dean, 1966). American negotiators found that the Chinese would struggle for days to establish a prejudicial, or "loaded," agenda in which the order of items discussed would be favorable to their tactical goals; or they would seek to phrase an agenda item so as to obtain at the outset the presumed end result of the negotiation (Joy, 1955). As one participant in this process concluded, "The characteristic feature of adversary negotiations with the Chinese Communists has been their manipulation of the agenda to place their opposites in an unfavorable trading position and to fix the substance of negotiations by the way an item is phrased or listed in the agenda" (Young, 1968, p. 379).

The experience of the normalization phase of U.S.-PRC relations was rather different in this regard, although Chinese negotiators, in less combative fashion, continued to pay close attention to the formulation of issues to be discussed:

> *The close rein on which Chinese negotiators are held, and the consequent need for extraordinarily meticulous advance preparation are indicated in the PRC's great attention to the question of the agenda for negotiations. Chinese representatives cannot function effectively if they are surprised by the content or sequence of discussions. They will therefore insist on the greatest possible amount of information on the other side's plans for conducting the talks in question. (Freeman, 1975, p. 12)*

The early, indirect contacts between the Nixon administration and the PRC involved delicate, yet pointed, exchanges on an agenda for direct discussions between senior leaders of the two sides. In these exploratory communications, the Chinese tried to focus the anticipated talks on the withdrawal of U.S. forces from Taiwan and establishment of U.S.-PRC diplomatic relations. The United States, for its part, attempted to define a much broader, open-ended agenda that would include discussion of global and regional security issues.

In the final exchanges via the Warsaw talks channel in early 1970, the Chinese negotiator, Lei Yang, again repeated his government's "principled position" that Taiwan was the crucial issue preventing an improvement in the U.S.-PRC relationship, but he made no demands on the United States and enticingly but ambiguously noted that it would be "necessary to create the conditions" to resolve the Taiwan issue as a matter of dispute between the two countries.[4] In an indirect message to the United States conveyed by the Rumanians a few months later, the Chinese rhetorically inquired how U.S.-PRC relations could improve if there were no withdrawal of U.S. forces from Taiwan.[5] Then, at the end of the year, the Pakistanis conveyed a message to the White House that was said to reflect the joint decision of Mao Zedong, Lin Biao, and Zhou Enlai to receive the president or his special envoy for talks in Beijing "in order to discuss the subject of the vacation [by U.S. forces] of Chinese territories called Taiwan."[6] The U.S. reply a few days later tried to keep

---

4. Stoessel-Lei, January 20 and February 20, 1970.

5. Rumanian Vice Premier Emil Bodnaras' briefing of U.S. Ambassador Leonard Meeker on July 14, 1970, after Bodnaras' return from a trip to China.

6. Kissinger-Hilaly, December 9, 1970.

the agenda open by saying, "The meeting in Peking [between U.S. and PRC leaders] would not be limited only to the Taiwan question but would encompass other steps designed to improve relations and reduce tensions."[7]

After some further delay, the Chinese sent their first formal message (as opposed to oral or indirect statements) to the administration, in which the Taiwan issue was referred to in only very general terms: "If the relations between China and the USA are to be restored fundamentally, a solution to this crucial question [of Taiwan] can only be found through direct discussions between high-level responsible persons of the two countries."[8] In his reply, President Nixon accepted Zhou's invitation to visit Beijing and added that during such a visit "each side would be free to raise the issue of principal concern to it."[9] Zhou confirmed this open-ended agenda, but then specified his own topic for discussion by asserting, "It goes without saying that the first question to be settled is the crucial issue between China and the United States which is the question of the concrete way of the withdrawal of all the U.S. armed forces from Taiwan and the Taiwan Strait area."[10]

With the establishment of direct U.S.-PRC contacts, the Chinese gradually escalated their demands regarding development of the bilateral relationship and pressed to keep the issues of Taiwan and normalization the only *public* topics of the discussions. During his first, secret trip to Beijing, Kissinger noted to Zhou that the premier was going beyond the issue of the withdrawal of U.S. military forces from Taiwan to include the question of diplomatic recognition;[11] and in drafting the first U.S.-PRC joint public

7. Kissinger-Hilaly, December 16, 1970.

8. Kissinger-Hilaly, April 27, 1971.

9. Kissinger-Hilaly, May 10, 1971.

10. Kissinger-Hilaly, May 29, 1971.

11. *Kissinger:* I have noticed that the Prime Minister in his remarks here went beyond some of the communications we have previously exchanged. Both in these communications and in our Warsaw meetings he has spoken of withdrawing military presence and installations from the area of Taiwan and the area of the Taiwan Strait. Today he has spoken also of certain official political declarations.

Zhou: This was because in order to exchange opinions one must give the entire opinion on the matter. (Zhou-Kissinger, July 9, 1971)

statement (issued on July 15, 1971, in the United States), Zhou sought to limit the announced topic of the forthcoming Nixon-Mao/Zhou meeting to the normalization of U.S.-PRC relations and to exclude reference to discussion of issues related to "Asian and world peace."[12] The final wording of the July 15 announcement bridged U.S. and Chinese objectives, yet toned down the implication that the two sides would discuss matters of international security and peace: "The meeting between the leaders of China and the United States is to seek the normalization of relations between the two countries and also to exchange views on questions of concern to the two sides" (Kissinger, 1979, pp. 759–760).

When they invited Kissinger to return to Beijing in October 1971, the Chinese stressed via the secret Paris channel that the purpose of the trip was "to seek normalization of relations" and asserted that "the talks should concentrate on the principal issue without diversion of attention to side issues."[13]

During the Nixon visit to Beijing, of course, issues of global and regional security, as well as the question of normalization of U.S.-PRC relations, were discussed. And the Shanghai Communiqué, issued on February 28, 1972, included the first joint Sino-American statement that "neither should seek hegemony in the Asia-Pacific region and each is opposed to efforts by any other country or group of countries to establish such hegemony." The agenda was set for continuing talks "to further the normalization of relations between the two countries and continue to exchange views on issues of common interest."[14] Yet it was only after the end of the Vietnam War in early 1973 that the Chinese became more open about their discussion of international security issues with the United States.

12. Zhou's effort to limit the announced agenda undoubtedly reflected PRC concerns about the reactions of its key allies, especially the North Koreans and North Vietnamese, to the secret Kissinger visit and the Nixon trip and about the way the Soviets would try to use the announcement to sow discord between the Chinese and their allies. (See Zhou-Kissinger, July 11, 1971.)

13. Walters-Huang Zhen, September 23, 1971.

14. See text of the Shanghai Communiqué in Solomon (1981), pp. 299–300.

With normalization on the agenda, the problem for the Chinese became that of how to move the United States to complete the process. President Nixon had expressed to Zhou Enlai in 1972 the intention to complete normalization in his second term; but when the Watergate scandal forced Nixon's resignation, the Chinese did not know whether President Ford would honor his predecessor's expression of intent. That issue came to a head in the summer of 1975 as Ford and Kissinger prepared for the second presidential visit to the PRC late in the year (which had been agreed to during Kissinger's November 1974 trip to Beijing).

The Chinese, in an effort to pressure the United States to consummate normalization, adopted throughout 1975 a passive-aggressive posture of unwillingness to put any other issues on the agenda of the forthcoming Ford visit. They knew that press attention to the trip, in the complex context of rising U.S.-Soviet tensions and the approach of the 1976 U.S. presidential election, would make the administration unusually anxious to keep some vitality in the U.S.-PRC relationship—and certainly concerned to avoid the appearance of deterioration in the relationship in the eyes of both the Soviets and the American public. Thus, the Chinese went into a mode of uncooperative passivity regarding the setting of agenda items for the visit. Kissinger and Liaison Office Chief Huang Zhen sparred inconclusively on agenda topics in meetings on May 9, July 7, and August 12; and Vice Premier Deng Xiaoping, turning to the media to build additional pressure on the administration, told a visiting delegation of American newspaper editors on June 2 that President Ford would be welcome in Beijing later in the year whether or not he had business to transact.[15]

Then, at a meeting in New York City with Foreign Minister Qiao Guanhua on September 28, Kissinger informed the Chinese

---

15. In one sense, Deng's statement took pressure *off* the president by saying, in effect, that it was not necessary for him to make progress on the normalization issue to be welcome in Beijing; and it kept the president locked into the visit. Yet Deng must have known that a presidential visit without any substance would be an embarrassment to the administration, since the Soviets would be sensitive to the state of the U.S.-PRC relationship, and the American press would be quick to interpret a substanceless presidential trip as a pre–election-year political ploy.

that normalization was politically impossible during the presidential visit. Qiao countered by replying to Kissinger's inquiry about substantive topics for a joint communiqué to be issued at the end of the presidential visit by saying that his mind was a blank. This session was followed by Kissinger's strained visit to Beijing in October, during which the Chinese leaders sharply attacked U.S. policies, stressed their own self-reliance, and rejected all U.S. offers for small steps forward in the relationship. In sum, the Chinese sought to confront the administration with the difficult choice of either a "successful" presidential visit based on completion of the normalization process, or the embarrassment of a trip with no agenda, in which the world would witness a stagnating U.S.-PRC relationship. (This is what in fact occurred in December, although the Chinese warmed up the mood of the visit somewhat, in comparison with the frosty reception accorded Kissinger in October.)

While the Chinese were not successful in pressuring the Ford administration into completing the normalization process, they continued to apply pressure on the issue by using an "if you won't talk about A, we won't talk about B" approach to agenda-setting on bilateral issues.

The Chinese also showed great reluctance to put items on a public agenda that might compromise their relations with their allies—especially the North Koreans, the Vietnamese (during the early 1970s), and the Khmer Communists. This was particularly evident in the spring of 1975 at the time of the *Mayaguez* crisis. On May 12, 1975, Deputy Secretary of State Robert Ingersoll called in Liaison Office Chief Huang Zhen and attempted to read to him an official demarche asking the PRC government to inform the newly victorious Khmer Communist government that if it did not release the *Mayaguez* and its crew, it would be responsible for the consequences. Huang Zhen, obviously acting on instructions from Beijing, cut off Ingersoll in the first part of his presentation, saying that the incident was an American problem and his government would not get involved even in the passing of a message to the new authorities in Phnom Penh.

In contrast to their approaches to keeping issues *off* an agenda, the Chinese can be tenacious in pressing for *inclusion* of issues. This was illustrated, in extreme form, during the adversarial negotiations at Panmunjom and Warsaw during the 1950s and 1960s. Later, in the normalization phase of Sino-U.S. negotiations, the Chinese persisted in "reserving position" on critical issues in order to reach at least partial agreements designed to draw the U.S. government deeper into a relationship.

High Principles (Versus High Demands)

> *We should not refuse to enter into negotiations because we are afraid of trouble and want to avoid complications, nor should we enter into negotiations with our minds in a haze. We should be firm in principle; we should also have all the flexibility permissible and necessary for carrying out our principles. (Mao Zedong, 1965, p. 372)*

> Deng Xiaoping: *If the U.S.-PRC relationship is to grow we must have a common principle, regardless of what political party is in power in the U.S. (Deng-Bush, May 8, 1982)*

A counterpoint to the Chinese emphasis on cultivating personal relationships as the basis for a negotiation is their stress on negotiating from a "principled" position. Rather than initiating a negotiating exchange with exaggerated demands from which they retreat in incremental compromises, the Chinese will press for acceptance of certain general principles, and only after these have been codified and the negotiating counterpart's position tested against them over an extended period of time will the Chinese move to conclude an agreement.

Henry Kissinger, among others, found this Chinese stress on principle to be quite different from the negotiating behavior of other nations. As he told President Nixon after his first encounter with Zhou Enlai, the Chinese "display an inward security that allows them, within the framework of their principles, to be meticulous and reliable in dealing with others" (Kissinger, 1979, p. 754). The Shanghai Communiqué was the result of the first year of normalization negotiations with the Chinese. Kissinger recalled that his initial draft of the document, which highlighted "fuzzy areas of agreement and obscured differences with platitudinous generalizations" (Kissinger, 1979, p. 781), had been rejected as an unacceptable, unprincipled way to proceed. Rather, the Chinese pressed for a document that sharply stated areas of disagreement as well as points of common interest. While jolted by the unaccustomed frankness of this way of constructing a joint communiqué, Kissinger noted that "as I reflected further I began to see that the very novelty of the approach might resolve our perplexities. A statement of differences would reassure allies and friends that their interests had been defended; if we could develop some common positions, these would then stand out as the authentic convictions of principled leaders" (Kissinger, 1979, p. 782).

While the accumulated record since the Shanghai Communiqué was negotiated shows that the Chinese are not always meticulous in dealings with others on the basis of their principles, and indeed that they may reach agreements that actually seem to violate the principles they stress in the early phases of a negotiation, they nonetheless predictably seek to engage negotiating counterparts in a commitment to certain generalized standards or objectives that form the basis for the pursuit of specific negotiating objectives. As one student of PRC negotiating behavior has observed:

> *In the vocabulary of PRC negotiators, goals which relate to long-range strategy are referred to as "principles" which must be rigidly adhered to, while goals which relate to short-range tactical advantage are referred to as "concrete arrangements" with regard to which they can be flexible . . . they concentrate on obtaining the agreement of the opposing side to the "principle" which they see as the main stake in the discussion, relegating to a secondary level of importance the "concrete arrangements" by which the "principle" is to be implemented. (Freeman, 1975, p. 6)*

Why do the Chinese lay such stress on principle? In some measure, it may be a reaction against the highly personalized quality of their policies—an effort to establish a substantive framework for a political relationship and to minimize the opportunism that is inherent in dealings based exclusively on personal relationships and self-interest. It also seems to reflect the Chinese need to know the political standpoint (*li-chang*) of a negotiating counterpart, especially a foreigner whose culture, political practice, and objectives are not clearly known and whose behavior is less subject to Chinese influence.

Above all, the stress on principle at the outset of a negotiation is an effective bargaining ploy in that it forces the counterpart government to accept (or reject) a very general commitment to a seemingly unobjectionable standard of behavior—such as the five principles of peaceful coexistence—which can then be used to constrain its room for bargaining through the accusation that certain actions or negotiating counters violate the general principle. It also provides a lofty and inflexible standard to which the PRC negotiator can rigidly and self-righteously adhere while he presses his counterpart to demonstrate in concrete terms that he really does accept his country's commitment to it.

In adversarial negotiations, PRC officials may rigidly put forward principled positions as a way of *preventing* movement toward an agreement. As Ambassador Jacob Beam recalled of his dealings with PRC officials at Warsaw in the late 1950s, "The Chinese . . . committed themselves to dogmatic and fixed positions which were non-negotiable. They rarely, if ever, changed their positions, letting them stand until they were obsolete, at which time they would substitute others equally non-negotiable" (Beam, 1978, pp. 111–112). The negotiating experience during the normalization process was rather different, however, for the Chinese saw their interests served by reaching agreements and building a relationship with the United States. Yet the record contains episodes of Chinese "principled rigidity," in which their officials have attempted to stall a negotiation or maneuver the U.S. side into accommodating to their principled position. For example, in 1978, as Beijing and Washington initiated the final phase of the normalization negotiations, Foreign Minister Huang Hua stressed to Liaison Office Chief Leonard Woodcock that the Taiwan issue remained the primary obstacle to full normalization, that the Chinese had been consistent in stating their "three principles" as the basis for completing the process, and that the Chinese side could go no further than its principled position in meeting U.S. concerns about its post-normalization relations with Taiwan.[16] A few months later, Huang conducted a virtual tirade against the U.S. position on normalization in a long dinner discussion with Secretary of State Vance in New York City, stressing the various

16. Huang Hua-Woodcock, July 7, 1978.

PRC principles that the United States had to accommodate to if normalization was to be accomplished.[17]

A foreign negotiator, of course, does not have to accept Chinese principles as a basis for negotiation—indeed, American negotiators at Warsaw refused for years to sign a joint statement of support for the five principles of peaceful coexistence or to accept the "principle" that all U.S. troops should be withdrawn from Taiwan. Such a refusal, of course, communicates that the foreign government is unwilling to build a relationship with the PRC on Chinese terms.

If a common basis in principle can be found, however, PRC negotiators can show considerable flexibility in the way it can be implemented, especially regarding the *timing* with which a commitment to principle is given concrete expression. Zhou said to Kissinger in 1972, in the context of a discussion of planned U.S. troop withdrawals from Taiwan during the year, "It doesn't matter whether you carry this [plan] out sooner or later because we have already fixed our principles during our discussion."[18]

PRC officials more frequently invoke principles to constrain the actions of their counterparts in areas affecting Chinese interests. As the Carter administration prepared to enter office in early 1977, for example, PRC Liaison Office Chief Huang Zhen invoked the principles of the Shanghai Communiqué as a basis for criticizing Carter's election-period characterization of Taiwan as a separate country and for keeping the new administration's China policy on the same track as that of its predecessors:

> *Huang Zhen: Frankly speaking, the Shanghai Communiqué constitutes the foundation of the present Sino-U.S. relationship and only if both sides strictly observe all the principles of the Shanghai Communiqué, then relations between our two countries can continue to be improved. Any action which goes back on the principles of the communiqué will result in harming the Sino-U.S. relationship.*
>
> *Vance: Let me say that I fully accept the principle of one China. . . .*
>
> *Huang Zhen: So we have no difficulty on this point.*[19]

17. Vance-Huang Hua, October 3, 1978.

18. Zhou-Kissinger, February 16, 1973.

19. Kissinger/Vance–Huang Zhen, January 8, 1977.

Accusations of violation of principle have been the primary Chinese plaint in attempts to pressure the United States to end its arms sales to Taiwan. In 1978, as normalization negotiations progressed, and as the Carter administration continued to sell arms to the island, PRC officials responded to each arms-sales announcement with complaints that the principles of the Shanghai Communiqué were being violated, belying the administration's expressions of serious intent to complete normalization of U.S.-PRC relations.

In the extreme, the Chinese are willing to challenge the basis for maintaining a cooperative relationship when they feel their principles are being violated by the other party.

Period of Assessment

Negotiating with the Chinese is almost invariably a protracted process. The U.S.-PRC ambassadorial talks at Geneva and Warsaw went on for 15 years, through 136 sessions, with only one concrete agreement being reached before the two sides saw their interests served by political normalization. The normalization negotiations themselves, beginning in the summer of 1971, persisted for more than seven years. Negotiation of the joint communiqué on arms sales to Taiwan in 1981–1982 went on for ten months, although the issue had been discussed by the two sides for years. And American businessmen, accustomed to negotiating in a culture in which time and efficiency are valuable assets, learn with frustration that "the first rule in negotiating with the Chinese is the need for abiding patience" (Pye, 1982, p. 49).

There are many mutually reinforcing reasons for the apparently desultory pace at which the Chinese pursue a negotiation: sluggish internal decisionmaking procedures; a willingness to reserve position on important issues until the most favorable political context presents itself; great sensitivity to the time rhythms of the political process as well as to the psychological benefits of having an impatient negotiating counterpart. At the core of this protracted process, however, is a compulsive need to have fully tested out the position of the other side before formulating and exposing one's own position. The greatest proportion of time in negotiations with the Chinese is consumed by their effort to draw out the counterpart official, to assess his or her motives and objectives, and to test out through a variety of facilitating maneuvers and pressure tactics the firmness of his or her position and degree of impatience to reach a settlement.

"Our Guests Always Speak First!"

When Henry Kissinger sat down for the first time across the green baize table from Zhou Enlai in the summer of 1971, the premier's first words were an almost ritualistic Chinese negotiating incantation: "According to our custom, we first invite our guest to speak. Besides, you have already prepared a thick [briefing] book. Of course, later on we will give our opinions also."[20]

Chinese officials seem virtually immune to pressures to present their own views before they believe their counterpart has laid out his or her position.[21] Secretary of State Vance, to his frustration, pressed Huang Hua for his views on normalization in 1977, only to get platitudes that were clearly irrelevant to serious negotiation on the subject. Leonard Woodcock, in his initial exchanges with Huang Hua on normalization in July 1978, proposed that the two sides alternate in presenting their views on a series of four issues that the United States wanted clarified as a basis for constructing a normalization agreement. The Chinese rejected this approach, saying that the U.S. side should present its position "comprehensively," in its entirety, before receiving a Chinese response.[22] And Secretary of Defense Harold Brown, on the second day of his visit to Beijing in 1980, invited his counterpart Geng Biao to present his views first, inasmuch as Geng was now meeting Brown in Brown's guest house. Geng retorted that as he was the host of Brown's entire visit it was most appropriate that Brown present his views first.[23] So ingrained is this ritual that Chinese officials, in unguarded moments, can

20. Zhou-Kissinger, July 9, 1971.

21. The one infrequent exception to this rule is the circumstance in which a Chinese negotiator wants to establish his principle as the basis for a discussion or has been instructed to lay out his side's position on an issue so as to delimit the bounds of a negotiation.

22. Huang Hua-Woodcock, July 5, 1978, and July 14, 1978.

23. Geng-Brown, January 7, 1980.

laugh about it with their American interlocutors—who almost invariably seem to defer to the Chinese custom:

> Qiao Guanhua: *Let's proceed as usual. I would like to take this opportunity to hear your views. Why don't you start?*
>
> Kissinger: *Because we are in your place tonight [I should go first] (laughter)!*
>
> Qiao: *We have two sayings: one is that when we are the host, we should let the guest begin; and the other is that when we are guests we should defer to the host.*
>
> Kissinger: *You can always use this so I have to start in any event (laughter). But I will be glad to start.*[24]

"Projective-Test" Diplomacy

The Chinese compulsion to get the other side to present its views first is one manifestation of a general approach to negotiating that might be characterized as projective-test diplomacy. Chinese negotiators will frequently put forward a vague but appropriate-sounding phrase—much like a Rorschach inkblot—as part of an exchange, leaving their counterpart to give concrete meaning to it, thus maneuvering him to develop a specific interpretation to which the Chinese side can then respond.

In some instances, the Chinese have used a vague but enticing phrase to draw the other side into a negotiation, without committing themselves to any specific solution. For example, in one of the key Warsaw talk exchanges of 1970 that led to initiation of the normalization dialogue, the Chinese asserted: "We are fully aware that the settlement of the Taiwan question requires making every effort to create the conditions."[25] What "creating the conditions" meant was not specified, yet the phrase contained a hint of flexibility on an issue where the Chinese had been "principled" and unyielding for two decades.

In the fall of 1973, PRC leaders apparently decided to try to accelerate the normalization process. Zhou Enlai inserted into the draft communiqué formulated at the end of Kissinger's sixth

24. Kissinger-Qiao, October 8, 1976.

25. Stoessel-Lei Yang, February 20, 1970.

visit to the PRC capital the vague but suggestive phrase, "Normalization can only be realized on the basis of confirming the principle of one China."[26] Exactly how the United States was expected to "confirm" this principle was not specified, yet an extensive, if delphic, discussion between Kissinger and Chairman Mao provided hints of possible approaches to completing the normalization process on the basis of doing so. As Kissinger and Zhou bantered after the session with Mao:

> Zhou: *. . . you mentioned earlier that we should use the wording of the Shanghai Communiqué to move the issue [of normalization] forward a bit. We have worked hard on one sentence in the text [of the draft communiqué] and you can examine it to see if it is useful or not.*
>
> Kissinger: *I have given a great deal of thought to our conversation and to the comments Chairman Mao made on Taiwan. As with all the things in my experience the Chairman says, there were many layers of meaning.*
>
> Zhou: *That is true.*
>
> Kissinger: *At least that was my impression. It was not a simple statement. And, therefore, I thought I should study his remarks for a brief time after I return and submit to you possible ideas.*[27]

In similar fashion, Mao put forward the notion that U.S.-PRC normalization had to follow the "Japan formula."[28] Apart from saying that the United States had to sever diplomatic relations with the authorities on Taiwan, the chairman's remarks did not further specify what the Japan formula involved. Yet this symbol was used by PRC leaders in the five ensuing years as the basis for discussions of approaches to normalization. Ultimately these exchanges led to a definition of the Japan formula that included, in addition to breaking diplomatic relations with Taiwan, the withdrawal of U.S. troops from the island and abrogation of the U.S.–Republic of China Mutual Defense Treaty—two conditions that had nothing to do with Japan's normalization arrangement with the PRC, as Japan had no troops on Taiwan and no defense treaty with the island. Yet the phrase "the Japan formula" or "the

---

26. Zhou-Kissinger, November 14, 1973.

27. Zhou-Kissinger, November 13, 1973.

28. Mao-Kissinger, November 12, 1973.

Japan model" served as a usefully vague symbol by which the Chinese attempted to draw out the United States over several years of discussion without limiting PRC room for maneuver on the issue.

Facilitating Maneuvers

The negotiating record of the 1970s and 1980s reveals a range of actions that can best be characterized as facilitating maneuvers —ploys to draw the counterpart government and its officials into a constructive relationship, to minimize confrontations (especially with senior leaders), and to preserve a positive working atmosphere in the context of problems which, if not handled with skill, could disrupt the relationship. We have already explored how the Chinese seek to manipulate the ambience of a negotiation to draw their foreign counterparts into a positive relationship; now, we describe other approaches they use to facilitate negotiating exchanges.

Intermediaries

Like other Asian cultures, the Chinese prefer to establish relationships by indirection, through the intercession of trusted intermediaries who can test out an unfamiliar or sensitive situation and convey intelligence on how to establish direct contact and how to minimize the chances of a confrontation that would jeopardize the development of a relationship.

The intermediation of Pakistani President Yahya Kahn played a particularly important role in laying the basis for direct contact between Chinese and American leaders in 1970–1971, as the Chinese tested out the intentions of the Nixon administration. In a November 1970 meeting, Zhou Enlai told the Pakistani president that he placed particular weight on Yahya's conveyance to him of a statement President Nixon had made to Yahya (in a September meeting in Washington). Nixon had said he was prepared to send a personal envoy to Beijing for meetings with Chinese leaders and that the United States would not form a condominium with the Soviet Union against China. Said Zhou to Yahya: "The United States knows that Pakistan is a great friend of China, and therefore we attach importance to the [Nixon] message."[29] And when Nixon finally met Mao in Beijing, the chairman told the president how important Yahya's intermediation had been in vouching for the sincerity of his indirect expressions of intent to normalize U.S.-PRC relations.

Some highly sensitive messages were passed through the Pakistani channel: Early on, the Chinese expressed concern that the United States would characterize China's interest in normalization as reflecting weakness or fear of U.S.-Soviet collusion against the PRC; and despite the continuing war in Vietnam, they expressed confidence that there was little possibility of a U.S.-PRC military conflict.[30] On the U.S. side, the Nixon administration emphasized via the Pakistanis that the United States would not collude with the Soviets against China; that strict secrecy was absolutely necessary for the establishment of direct communications; and that President Nixon hoped the PRC would refrain from inviting other American political figures to China until after a presidential visit.[31] As noted above, the two sides also bargained over an agenda for their direct talks via the Pakistani link.

The Chinese took great care in choosing intermediaries whom they felt they could rely upon. The Pakistanis were the most trusted of the governments they (and the United States) turned to for reliable and secure communications in the 1970–1971 period. They used with considerably more reserve the Rumanian leaders who were entrusted by the Nixon administration to pass to PRC leaders expressions of interest in normalization. In the first year of the Nixon administration, the United States asked Rumania to convey a letter to Zhou Enlai from American journalist Theodore White expressing his desire to visit China at a time when the U.S. government, to which he said he had access at the highest level, was rethinking its Asia policy. The Chinese never responded to this approach, preferring instead to use their "old friend" Edgar Snow to convey their views on normalization in the fall of 1970 via a series of senior-leadership interviews—

---

29. Kissinger-Hilaly, December 9, 1970; and Nixon-Yahya Kahn, October 15, 1970.

30. Kissinger-Hilaly, February 26, 1970.

31. Nixon-Yahya Kahn, October 25, 1970; Kissinger-Hilaly, April 28, 1971, and May 10, 1971.

and the symbolic touch of a highly visible reception of Snow by Chairman Mao atop Tian An Men on China's national day (October 1).

While there is a certain measure of randomness in PRC selection of intermediaries—depending on who is available when the PRC wishes to send an indirect communication—it appears that the trust of *guanxi,* high-level access in Washington, and shared political views and interests are the primary qualifications for intermediary status.

The Chinese used intermediaries not only for reestablishing direct U.S.-PRC communication in the early 1970s, but also in subsequent periods when they wanted to convey to the U.S. government particularly sensitive messages in a deniable manner, or when their relations with a particular administration were not very good—when *guanxi* was lacking. In the summer and fall of 1975, when they were anxious to complete normalization before the 1976 U.S. presidential elections, the Chinese again turned to the Pakistanis to convey a sense of their growing impatience at the lack of progress on the issue. In the same period, the hospitalized Zhou Enlai received a Chinese-American doctor who had been a schoolmate of Chairman Mao's to convey the message to the Ford administration that Beijing would be prepared to make a statement for domestic consumption about its intention to use only peaceful means in dealing with Taiwan if the United States would normalize relations according to the Japan formula.[32]

Indirect Communications

A variation on the Chinese use of intermediaries is the use of various forms of indirect communication as a way to avoid confrontations with senior authorities, to facilitate the exchange of ideas in a negotiating situation without formal commitment, or to probe or influence the attitudes of counterpart officials.

The Chinese have a very strong impulse to avoid direct confrontations between senior leaders, especially when a relationship

---

32. Personal recollection of the author.

is judged worthy of protection and cultivation. A clear example of this was the 1981 meeting between President Reagan and Premier Zhao Ziyang at Cancun, Mexico, in the context of tensions between the two countries over the issue of U.S. arms sales to Taiwan. Lower-level PRC officials had primed the administration for the encounter by telling both Secretary of State Alexander Haig and National Security Adviser Richard Allen that Zhao would "touch on" the issue of American arms sales to Taiwan, that Foreign Minister Huang Hua would make important contributions to the discussion, and that Huang would subsequently come to Washington to work out a complete solution to the issue.[33] During the Cancun meeting, Zhao touched only briefly on the arms-sales issue, devoting his attention instead to a presentation on the PRC's recently published nine-point program for peaceful reunification with Taiwan and his government's peaceful intentions toward the island. At the end of his remarks, however, Zhao said that because he had run out of time, Foreign Minister Huang Hua would later convey to him via Secretary of State Haig two important points on the arms-sales issue.[34] Two days later, Huang Hua, emphasizing that he was speaking on behalf of Zhao, pressed Haig on the issue.

This highly orchestrated episode illustrates how the Chinese will seek to facilitate communication of bargaining demands to a leadership with which they do not have intimate relations in a manner that minimizes direct confrontation between senior officials, and their use of an official they consider to be friendly (in this case, Haig) as a channel of communication.

In similar fashion, the Chinese sought to minimize tensions with President Carter in 1978, during the negotiations on the normalization agreement, by directing their protests on U.S. arms sales to Taiwan to the Department of State at the assistant secretary level, rather than to the White House—a pattern the Carter administration characterized as "the complaint channel."

The Chinese also use indirect, lower-level communications when they want to trade ideas in a noncommittal manner (and

33. Haig-Zhang Wenjin, September 22, 1981; Allen-Chai, October 2, 1981.

34. Reagan-Zhang, October 21, 1981.

shape the thinking of the other side) prior to the joining of the issue by senior negotiators "on the record." At the beginning of the negotiations on arms sales, Vice Foreign Minister Zhang Wenjin invited his counterpart, Ambassador Arthur Hummel, to meet with him periodically over informal luncheons to exchange ideas relating to the negotiation informally and "without commitment."[35] This pattern of mealtime communication persisted throughout the negotiation, with participation eventually shifting to the deputies of the principal negotiators, via whom the Chinese communicated sensitive messages that they did not wish to have in the record.[36]

PRC officials also use lower-level contacts to probe and test the state of play of a negotiation or to put forward negotiating positions in a deniable or low-key manner so as to maintain flexibility and minimize the sense that they are anxious to attain a particular result. In 1974, PRC leaders had lower-level operatives nudge their U.S. Liaison Office counterparts on the normalization issue—but not in a manner that would make them appear anxious for consummation of the process. In June of that year, a U.S. Liaison Office official was approached by a Foreign Ministry counterpart who voiced concern about Secretary of State Kissinger's preoccupation with issues other than China policy; and in the fall, on the eve of Kissinger's seventh visit to Beijing, Nancy Tang rhetorically inquired of Liaison Office Chief George Bush whether Kissinger's stated normalization strategy of "gaining time" to build political support in the United States for the China relationship hadn't become an end in itself (i.e., just a delaying tactic).[37] Similarly, the ever-present Foreign Ministry official Lian Zhengbao, while assigned to the PRC Liaison Office in Washington, approached an NSC official in November 1978—when the normalization negotiation was at a "now-or-never" phase—and said that in response to an inquiry from the U.S. side, Chinese leaders *would* be available in December for a

35. Zhang-Hummel, December 4, 22, 1981.

36. It should be noted that this pattern of off-the-record, informal exchanges is not unique to the Chinese. The same pattern in U.S.-Soviet arms-control negotiations is described in Talbot (1984), especially Chap. 6.

37. Kissinger-Huang Zhen, November 11, 1974.

meeting with American leaders. (In fact, no such inquiry had been made by the U.S. side!)

Ambiguous but Loaded Language

Another Chinese approach to communicating sensitive political messages is the use of ambiguous but loaded forms of expression, often in informal contexts such as mealtime banter or sightseeing excursions. We have already noted how Mao Zedong and Zhou Enlai obliquely hinted to Henry Kissinger about political conflict within the top leadership. And Zhou (who became so ill with cancer in 1974 that he had to withdraw from active political life) seems to have hinted to President Nixon in 1972 that he had serious health problems—in part, as a way of urging Nixon to follow through expeditiously on his stated intention to complete the normalization process in his second term:

> Zhou (in the context of a discussion of India): *At the time I hadn't read [Nehru's book* The Discovery of India], *but my late colleague Chen Yi had, and called it to my attention. . . .*
>
> Nixon: *When did Chen Yi die?*
>
> Zhou: *Just recently. Chairman Mao attended the funeral. He [Chen] had cancer of the stomach. Do you have a way of curing cancer?*
>
> Nixon: *It is a serious problem. One of the programs we want to undertake this year is a massive research program on cancer. . . .*
>
> Zhou: *We can cooperate in that field. . . .*
>
> . . . .
>
> Zhou: . . . *In your [guest house] dining room upstairs we also have a poem by Chairman Mao in his own calligraphy about Lushan Mountain, the last sentence of which reads, "The beauty lies at the top of the mountain." You have also risked something to come to China. There is another Chinese poem which reads: "On perilous peaks dwells beauty in its infinite variety."*
>
> Nixon: *We are at the top of the mountain now [Chinese laugh].*
>
> Zhou: *That's one poem. Another one which I would have liked to put up, but I couldn't find an appropriate place, is "Ode to a Plum Blossom." I had an original plan to take you to see the plum blossoms in Hangchow, but I have heard that their time has already passed. They are ahead of season this year.*
>
> Kissinger: *They have passed already?*

> Zhou: *I don't know why. In other years they have not shed so early. In that poem, the Chairman meant that one who makes an initiative may not always be the one who stretches out his or her hand [to receive the benefit]. By the time the blossoms are full blown, that is the time they are about to disappear. . . .*
>
> Nixon: *That's very beautiful.*
>
> Zhou: *Therefore, we believe we are in accord with the idea you just expressed. You are the one who made the initiative. You may not be there to see its success, but of course we would welcome your return. . . . I was only trying to illustrate the Chinese way of thinking. It does not matter anyhow. Regardless of who is the next President, the spirit of '76 still exists and will prevail. From the standpoint of policies I hope that our [American] counterparts will be the same so we can continue our efforts. We also hope not only that the President [Nixon] continues in office but that your adviser [Kissinger] and assistants continue in office. For example, if I should suddenly die of a fatal heart attack, you would also have to find another counterpart. Therefore, we try to bring more people to meet you. At least the interpreters have the hope of living longer than the Prime Minister.*[38]

Zhou also communicated sensitive policy messages in this oblique form. In 1972, he and Kissinger had months of exchanges on the issue of how to deal with the Cambodian conflict, with Zhou urging Kissinger to deal with Prince Sihanouk and his Royal Government of National Union (RGNU) coalition (which was dominated by the Communist Khmer Rouge forces). As the military situation deteriorated in favor of the insurgents, Congress withdrew support for American involvement in the conflict by mandating an end to the U.S. bombing campaign against the Communist forces. In this situation, Kissinger at last indicated a willingness to deal with Sihanouk—while also communicating to the PRC premier his expectation that the Chinese side would work with the United States to construct a Sihanouk-led coalition government that would not be dominated by the Communist forces. When Congress voted to stop the U.S. bombing campaign, the American side of this complex equation lost its capacity to influence events. Zhou obliquely communicated Kissinger's powerlessness to him by inviting him to Beijing for talks on August 16—the first day of the congressionally imposed bombing

38. Zhou-Nixon, February 23, 1972.

halt. By proposing one specific date, the premier signaled that the U.S. side had undercut its ability to influence the Cambodian situation and that Kissinger's trip to Beijing would be of no avail.[39]

In 1978, when the Chinese wished to accelerate the normalization negotiations, they did so in a way that would minimize the impression that they were anxious for a settlement. Among the oblique signals they sent was Foreign Minister Huang Hua's remark to Secretary of State Cyrus Vance in response to Vance's statement that Liaison Office Chief Leonard Woodcock would shortly begin formal discussions in Beijing on a normalization agreement:

> *In a dinner hosted by Vice Premier Deng in Bei Hai Park, they [Deng and Brzezinski] conducted a very interesting conversation [on the normalization issue]. Vice Premier Deng said that in another three years he may declare his retirement as he is getting advanced in age. With regard to the invitation extended by Dr. Brzezinski for the Vice Premier to make a visit to the United States, the Vice Premier said: "In that case we must work harder, since I am getting old."*[40]

Deng himself has been a master of the oblique-yet-pointed form of communication. There is a classical Chinese expression, "Pointing at the mulberry to revile the locust" (*zhi-sang ma-huai*), which means making indirect or oblique accusations. This was the initial form of public disputation between the Chinese and the Soviets in the early 1960s, when they attacked surrogate figures to minimize the impact of their developing feud—the Soviets publicly criticized the Albanians by name, while the Chinese attacked the Yugoslavs—rather than criticizing each other directly.

The Chinese used a similar form of criticism to minimize the corrosive effect on the U.S.-PRC relationship of their public attacks on American foreign policies. The clearest example of this tactic is Deng's criticism, in 1975–1980, of détente with the Soviet Union. Rather than directly accusing the Nixon, Ford, and Carter administrations of appeasing the Soviets, Deng and other senior PRC officials publicly and privately attacked the "Munich

---

39. This complex period of history is detailed in Kissinger (1982), pp. 339–369.

40. Vance-Huang Hua, June 2, 1978.

mentality" which they said was still prevalent in "the West" (not further specified).[41]

Another example of the oblique approach to presenting a sensitive message is Defense Minister Geng Biao's recitation of the history of Sino-Soviet relations for Secretary of State Edmund Muskie and other officials during his visit to Washington in the spring of 1980. Geng wished to communicate to the Carter administration—with which the Chinese hoped to develop a defense relationship—the object lesson of how (according to the Chinese) the Soviets had mismanaged their security assistance program with the PRC (one of the major causes of the Sino-Soviet feud). It was also an oblique way of saying to the Americans that the break with Moscow was irreparable (and therefore the United States could trust China as a reliable security partner who would not double-cross it by turning back to the Soviets).[42]

The usually subtle and sophisticated Chinese are not above the occasional personal dig at a foreign leader; yet even such lapses of political discipline are usually expressed obliquely:

> Deng Xiaoping (to Secretary of State Haig): *How is Dr. Kissinger?*
>
> Haig: *He is well. I spoke to him just before I left [Washington]. He had just come back from Europe.*
>
> Deng: *I am very familiar with Dr. Kissinger. And we have great admiration for Mr. Nixon.*[43]

Self-Deprecation

Another form of discourse used by the Chinese to signal their interest in cultivating a relationship is self-criticism and self-deprecation—a tactic that is all the more notable in view of their underlying pride and self-confidence. Richard Nixon was impressed in 1972 by his hosts' obsession with self-criticism and their apparent lack of conceit and arrogance, in contrast to the Soviets, who, Nixon noted, always insist that their achievements

41. See, for example, Deng's discussion of détente with President Ford, December 2, 1975.

42. Muskie-Geng Biao, May 28, 1980.

43. Deng-Haig, June 16, 1981.

are the biggest and the best (Nixon, 1978, pp. 570–578; Kissinger, 1979, pp. 1056, 1081). Mao responded to Nixon's flattering observation about the impact of his writings and political sloganeering by characterizing their impact as little more than "firing empty cannons":

> Nixon: *The Chairman's writings moved a nation and have changed the world.*
>
> Mao: *I haven't been able to change it. I've only been able to change a few places in the vicinity of Beijing.*[44]

And like the self-critical Zhou Enlai, who sought to defuse an American reporter's criticism of some sightseeing arrangements during the Nixon presidential visit with a forthright admission of error, Deng Xiaoping also sought to preempt complaint with self-criticism. The following exchange took place between Deng and Liaison Office Chief George Bush in October 1975:

> Deng: *There is one thing we should apologize for. A few days ago one of our sentries at the Liaison Office kept out one of [Ambassador Bush's] guests, due to lack of knowledge of diplomatic affairs. We should take this occasion to apologize.*
>
> Bush: *That is very gracious of you. It was a small matter. . . .*
>
> Deng: *We should apologize.*[45]

Humor

A number of the American officials interviewed for this study remarked on the easy rapport they developed with their Chinese counterparts and the humor that can characterize exchanges across the negotiating table when the overall relationship has a positive mood. Kissinger noted in his memoirs the "easy comradery not untinged with affection" that he had developed with Zhou Enlai after five visits to the PRC, and he drew from the record of his exchanges with the Chinese premier an example of the relaxed humor that seems to develop easily between Americans and Chinese:

> Kissinger: *I think that the Prime Minister notices that I am especially inhibited in his presence right now.*

---

44. Mao-Nixon, February 21, 1972.

45. Deng-Kissinger, October 19, 1975.

Zhou: *Why?*

Kissinger: *Because I read his remarks to the press that I am the only man who can talk to him for a half hour without saying anything.*

Zhou: *I think I said one hour and a half. (Kissinger, 1982, p. 46)*

In contrast to the heavy and often violence-tinged humor invoked by Soviet officials, the Chinese tend to display subtle and intellectually deft humor in circumstances where they wish to express a positive mood or to twit their American counterparts—a style that makes the contrasting episodes of calculated insult when they wish to bring pressure on their interlocutors all the more effective. Vice Foreign Minister Qiao Guanhua, Kissinger's counterpart in negotiating the Shanghai Communiqué, good-naturedly needled Kissinger in late 1972 for his tendency to forget or block Qiao's name—as evidenced by his periodic references to Qiao by the awkwardly formal title "Mr. Vice Foreign Minister." As Qiao toasted Kissinger at a dinner in New York:

> *In the past two years, in the improvement of relations between China and the United States, all people will remember one person without a name who is here tonight—"Mr. Doctor"—who has made outstanding contributions. And we hope that in the relations between our two countries we will continue to overcome various obstacles and difficulties and head toward accelerated normalization. At this time I would like to express congratulations on the reelection of President Nixon. I agree with the views of our many friends, and our friend whose name I forgot. Therefore, I propose a toast to the man whose name I forgot, to Mr. Governor [Rockefeller], and to all our friends and the great people of our two countries, and to our great friendship.*[46]

Playing Dumb (Calculated Misunderstanding)

The Chinese are clearly intelligent and highly calculating—especially in their political relations. Indeed, Henry Kissinger frequently played to their pride and humor with the self-deprecating observation that by Chinese standards he was only of average intelligence (Kissinger, 1979, p. 778). The high level of intelligence they bring to the negotiating process thus makes episodes in which they "play dumb" in order to elide issues they do not wish to see joined all the more evident as a facilitating tactic.

46. Kissinger-Qiao, November 13, 1972.

Provocation

The Chinese clearly understand the uses of relatively passive stratagems for facilitating a negotiation, and they also show an awareness of how provocations can create an environment in which negotiations can be moved forward. A provocation can be an effective way of building pressure on a counterpart—as we will explore below, in the section on pressure tactics—but in a political environment of multiple actors such as the triangular relations that existed among China, the Soviet Union, and the United States, a provocation toward one can help move the other into a more favorable position in terms of Chinese interests.

This was the dynamic of great-power relations in the late 1960s, when Sino-Soviet relations had deteriorated to a point of military confrontation, with the Soviets pressing a buildup of forces on China's northern frontier. After Moscow's invasion of Czechoslovakia in the summer of 1968, the Chinese feared that Soviet leaders had few inhibitions left about taking military action against the PRC, which they would justify in terms of Brezhnev's doctrine of the limited sovereignty of socialist states.

In this context, the problem for the virulently anti-Soviet Mao Zedong was how to cope with the growing Soviet military threat: either by the self-imposed isolation of the Cultural Revolution (during which China had withdrawn all but one of its ambassadors from abroad, and had as virtually its sole ally little Albania), or through an as-yet unformed coalition of states similarly threatened by Moscow's "new Tsars." Mao and Zhou also had the tactical problem of how to respond to Moscow's inclination to use displays of military force to intimidate their adversaries. To show fear would only play into Soviet hands; yet China was not strong enough militarily to cope with a direct Soviet attack, either nuclear or conventional, except through a costly and protracted "people's war."

The history of the years 1969–1971 suggests that Mao decided on a strategy of provocation to force the Soviets to face up to the reality of a Sino-Soviet war, to signal his unwillingness to be intimidated, and to highlight to other states similarly threatened by the Soviets their common cause in dealing with the aggressive leadership in the Kremlin. His vehicle for provoking the Soviets was a controlled application of force on a desolate and frozen border island where Chinese and Russian forces patrolled contested territory, Zhen Bao Island in China's northeastern province of Heilongjiang. The initial firefight of March 2, 1969, seems to have been at China's initiative (Robinson, 1970), with the Soviets responding to the provocation on March 15 with a massive use of force on a local scale.

The political effect of this overt, if limited, warfare between the two giants of the communist world was to give Mao a vehicle for mobilizing his population for a possibly expanded conflict with the Soviets, and an issue with which to appeal for common cause with the East Europeans, who only recently had felt (again) the blade of Soviet military intervention, in Czechoslovakia.

If one assumes that Mao also had in mind the objective of building a broader international coalition against the Soviet Union—one that would even include the United States (Nixon had been signaling his interest in a new relationship with China since his 1967 *Foreign Affairs* article)—then Mao's provocation was successful, at least to the extent that it gained Washington's attention.[47] As Kissinger recalled in his memoirs, "The Sino-Soviet border clashes of 1969 had first alerted us to the desirability of restoring contact with Beijing" (Kissinger, 1982, p. 46).

Mao continued to reveal his instinct for provocative stratagems as a way of influencing the play of the strategic triangle when the U.S.-PRC dialogue began. One of the first issues raised by Zhou Enlai during Kissinger's secret visit to Beijing in July 1971 was whether Nixon, apart from his willingness to come to China, was planning a summit meeting with Soviet leaders. Zhou clearly expressed his preference that Nixon visit the Soviet Union first,

47. Zhou said to Kissinger in 1973 in a critique of détente, "The strategic principle should be to expose that [the Soviets] are for general expansion and for false relaxation. For the past years we have never ceased in exposing the Soviet Union's expansionism and their false relaxation. We have done this since the Chen Pao incident in 1969" (Zhou-Kissinger, February 17, 1973).

as "we would not want to deliberately create tensions."[48] On the last day of Kissinger's visit, however, Zhou reversed his position, saying that Chairman Mao personally had decided "that it might be convenient to your needs if maybe the President's visit was earlier and not necessarily in the spring [of 1972]." And as the premier correctly noted, "Once the announcement [of the Nixon trip] is made it will shake the world, which won't be able to sleep."[49] Mao apparently had decided, upon reflection, that the risks of provoking the Soviets to take action against China because of the opening of the Sino-American dialogue were not as great as the possible benefits to be gained by stirring up distrust and tensions between Moscow and Washington, thus preventing Soviet-American collusion against the PRC.

Throughout the few remaining years of his life, Mao continued to display a penchant for using provocative maneuvers to influence U.S. policy, even to the point of playing on presumed interpersonal rivalries within the U.S. government. In November 1974, the recently rehabilitated Deng Xiaoping, undoubtedly acting on the chairman's instructions, shocked Kissinger by inviting his presumed rival, Secretary of Defense James Schlesinger, to China:

> Deng: *We have another consideration about the relations between our two countries. That is, as I have said before, some people have been saying the relations between our two countries have been cooling down. The Chinese government is therefore extending an invitation to you. That is to say, the Chinese government wishes to extend a formal invitation to the Secretary of Defense of the United States, Mr. Schlesinger, to visit China. We think this would be a good answer to all these opinions which are going on in the world.*
>
> Kissinger: *It will produce a Politburo meeting in the Kremlin.*
>
> Deng: *We don't mind. Well, actually it is our wish that they have a Politburo meeting there. But we really extend this invitation with all seriousness.*[50]

A year later, Mao was still using the Schlesinger invitation to needle Kissinger, expressing his unhappiness with the U.S. pol-

48. Zhou-Kissinger, July 10, 1971.

49. Zhou-Kissinger, July 11, 1971.

50. Deng-Kissinger, November 26, 1974.

icy of détente and Washington's favorable occupation of the "swing" position in the strategic triangle:

> Mao: *Please send my regards to your Secretary of Defense.*
>
> Kissinger: *I will do that.*
>
> Mao: *I am dissatisfied that he went to Japan without coming to Beijing. We want to invite him here for the Soviets to see, but you are too miserly. The U.S. is so rich, but on this you are too miserly.*
>
> Kissinger: *We can discuss it when the President [Ford] is here.*
>
> Mao: *Bring him [Schlesinger] along. You can bring a civilian and a military member with your President, both a civilian and a military man.*
>
> Kissinger: *Me as the civilian and Schlesinger as the military?*
>
> Mao: *Yes. But I won't interfere in your internal affairs. It is up to your side to decide whom you will send.*
>
> Kissinger: *Well, he will not come with the President. Maybe later.*[51]

That the Chairman's invitation to Schlesinger was for political effect, both on the Soviets and within the U.S. administration, was made clear by his rejection, in the same conversation, of any functional discussion of U.S.-PRC military cooperation:

> Kissinger: *We have tried to suggest to you that we are prepared to advise or help in some of these [defense] problems.*
>
> Mao: *As for military aspects, we should not discuss that now. Such matters should wait until the war breaks out before we consider them.*[52]

Stalling

The Chinese are extremely sensitive to the time rhythms of the negotiating process and to the ways in which domestic and international factors play on a political relationship. They have shown great skill at pacing a negotiation so that issues are not joined when circumstances are unfavorable to their objectives—just as they try to accelerate discussions when they feel time and conditions are ripe for reaching a favorable solution. The

---

51. Mao-Kissinger, October 21, 1975.

52. Mao-Kissinger, October 21, 1975.

Chinese used a stalling strategy during their dispute with the United States on the Taiwan issue in the 1950s and 1960s. A Chinese internal military document of 1961 explicitly stated:

> *It is better to maintain a frozen relationship between China and the United States, with a continued impasse for many years. If this problem [of Taiwan] is to be settled, we want to do so all at once. . . . Up to the present time we can see no expression of relaxation concerning Sino-American relations or any sign of sincerity. This is why we say that the unbending attitude is found on the side of the United States, and not on the side of China. Of course, the far-reaching view of the relationship between the two countries is optimistic and some day this problem will arrive at a satisfactory solution.*[53]

In the normalization negotiations of the 1970s, the Chinese seem to have purposefully stalled serious discussion of issues to prevent their coming to a head at an unfavorable time for the PRC on two occasions. In the summer of 1977, Secretary of State Vance traveled to Beijing to initiate discussions on behalf of President Carter. Vance's strategy, in part, was to raise issues such as the need for a U.S. post-normalization presence on Taiwan, in order to get certain positions on the record as much as to gain immediate agreement (although he did have a draft normalization communiqué in his pocket). Vance's counterpart was Vice Premier Deng Xiaoping, only recently resurrected from his third purging (which had occurred in the spring of 1976, sixteen months earlier), who shared leadership responsibilities uneasily with Mao's chosen successor, Hua Guofeng. In these circumstances, Deng and other leaders listened to Vance's presentation on the normalization issue and then attacked it as a "step backward" from the position expressed by President Ford and Secretary of State Kissinger during their visit to China in December 1975. They put off further discussion of the issue by urging the United States to take its time in seriously thinking through the PRC's position on normalization (Oksenberg, 1982, p. 183).

The Chinese continued to stall on normalization throughout 1977, despite continuing probes by U.S. officials. Foreign Minister

53. "Secret Instructions to the Chinese Army" (April 25, 1961), in Subcommittee on National Security and International Operations (1969), p. 78.

Huang Hua said to Liaison Office Chief Leonard Woodcock at the end of one session in November: "We hope we can take time and discuss these questions at an appropriate time. But we don't ask the U.S. side to give us an immediate reply. If at present you are unable to give us a new formula we can wait and continue our discussions later."[54]

From the PRC's perspective, this stalling posture not only avoided discussion of the issue in an unfavorable political context, it also put the United States under further pressure by rejecting the Vance presentation and forcing the American side to come up with additional—and presumably more favorable—proposals. It was only in the summer of 1978, when Deng had further consolidated his domestic political position and was anticipating a confrontation with Vietnam and the Soviet Union over Cambodia, that the Chinese began to press for action on normalization.

The Chinese similarly stalled the negotiation on a communiqué regarding U.S. arms sales to Taiwan for a period in the spring of 1982, apparently because of conflicts within the leadership on how to deal with the issue. The Chinese held rigidly to their position in a series of emotional and uncompromising presentations in March of that year,[55] yet prior and subsequent asides by several Foreign Ministry officials to their U.S. counterparts about the state of play of their leadership conveyed the impression that their rigidity reflected a purposeful effort by the Foreign Ministry to stall the talks in a context of internal political disarray.

Reserving Position

A rather distinctive Chinese stratagem for facilitating a negotiation is to assert a principled position on problems that cannot be readily resolved and then proceed to reach a partial agreement on resoluble issues. In this way they gain partial objectives and draw the counterpart government into a more positive relationship, while maintaining their position on the intractable problems for resolution at some future time in a more favorable context.

54. Huang Hua-Woodcock, November 14, 1977.

55. Pu Shouchang-Hummel, March 18, 1982; Zhang Zai-Freeman, March 22, 1982; Pu Shouchang-Freeman, March 24, 1982.

The tactic of reserving position seems to find particular use during the agreement-making phase of a negotiation, when the Chinese have tested the position of their adversary and have concluded that resolving certain aspects of an issue, while holding off on other aspects, will serve their purposes. We will come back to this tactic in the discussion of the end-game phase of the negotiating process.

Backing Off (Redefining Demands)

Much of the record of U.S.-PRC negotiations on normalization shows each side seeking to define in concrete terms the basis for establishing a positive relationship within the bounds of certain general national objectives or principles. The Chinese, despite the purposefulness and skill of their negotiators, do not seem to have had a highly specified game plan for these negotiations; rather, they seem to have felt their way through protracted discussions at a general level, using suggestive statements of purpose and principle to draw out the U.S. side and then, in the concluding phase of the negotiations, defining an agreement in the specific terms of a joint public document.

While there are numerous examples of Chinese officials backing off their initial demands in *commercial* negotiations to save an agreement, PRC leaders go to considerable lengths to maintain their credibility in *political* negotiations by *not* putting themselves in a position of having to back away from their initially stated demands. The Chinese place great importance on the credibility of their word and their negotiators.

Leave a Way Out

One of the military stratagems of *Sun-tzu* is to leave one's adversary a way out *(chu-lu)* in battle, so that he will not be forced to fight to the death. Likewise, in Chinese negotiations, PRC officials attempt to present the appearance of being absolutely unyielding on an issue, yet they will use wording that leaves open the possibility of reaching a compromise agreement.

Pressure Tactics

The Chinese use an even more diverse set of approaches to build pressure on a counterpart government in order to move a negotiation in a direction that is favorable to PRC interests. Pressure tactics used in recent years can be broadly categorized into the style of argumentation invoked by PRC officials and structural aspects of the negotiating process that Chinese officials seek to manipulate. The latter category includes various forms of political pressure the Chinese seek to bring into play.

Playing Adversaries Against Each Other

The U.S.-PRC negotiating record during the normalization process shows a recurring impulse on the part of the Chinese to build pressure by playing their negotiating counterparts' adversaries against them. This was evident in the early encounters in 1971, when PRC leaders let the Nixon administration know that if progress was not made, they could turn to numerous political figures in the Democratic party who were eager to visit China. Zhou Enlai told Kissinger on his first trip to Beijing:

> Zhou: *You can see [there are] a lot of politicians we have not invited to come here. I have a great pile of letters from them on my desk asking for invitations, which I have not answered.*
>
> Kissinger: *What you have done is greatly appreciated by President Nixon.*
>
> Zhou: *This is done under the instruction and wisdom of Chairman Mao.*[56]

The premier, by his understated remark, sought to gain credit for restraint in not responding to these requests, while keeping alive the possibility of a change in Chairman Mao's "wise" policy regarding dealing with the opposition. Indeed, Mao said to Nixon in February 1972, "As for the Democratic party, if they come into office again, we cannot avoid contacting them."[57] But as Zhou had already told Kissinger, he and Mao believed that Nixon's shift in China policy would in fact contribute to the president's reelection—and thus, by dealing with Nixon alone, they would put the president in their debt.[58]

---

56. Zhou-Kissinger, July 10, 1971.
57. Mao-Nixon, February 21, 1972.
58. Zhou-Kissinger, July 9, 1971.

PRC leaders have been less reserved about playing political rivals *of the same party* against each other. As noted earlier, Deng Xiaoping's invitation to Secretary of Defense James Schlesinger in November 1974 was used to twit Kissinger throughout his tenure as Secretary of State. The following byplay took place between Kissinger and Liaison Office Chief Huang Zhen in the summer of 1976:

> Kissinger: *You have had many visitors. I think you will have many visitors in September, won't you?*
>
> Huang Zhen: *To whom are you referring?*
>
> Kissinger: *I think Senator Mansfield is going; and I understand that my former colleague Schlesinger will be inspecting your fortifications during September.*
>
> Huang Zhen: *He will not be making an inspection; rather he has asked to get around the country, and we are trying to accommodate him. Moreover, Senator Mansfield will go to even more places.*
>
> Kissinger: *I don't object.*
>
> Huang Zhen: *You remember that we invited him [Schlesinger] in 1974. Don't be jealous. You have been to China nine times I believe. You even said yourself you wanted to go to Inner Mongolia.*
>
> Kissinger: *But I didn't get there. I wanted to see the musk ox of Mongolia.*[59]

In similar fashion, the Chinese used invitations to Nixon and members of his family in the fall of 1975 to pressure President Ford on normalization as he prepared for his own trip to the PRC. And they encouraged President Carter's national security adviser, Zbigniew Brzezinski, against his rumored rival Secretary of State Vance when they were urging the Carter administration to adopt a harder line against the Soviet Union and to make progress in the normalization negotiations in 1978.

Chinese leaders were also highly sensitive to the play of Soviet-American relations and their own strained dealings with the USSR as they affected the PRC's position within the "strategic

---

59. Kissinger-Huang Zhen, August 18, 1976. See also Huang Zhen's use of Schlesinger's public criticism of détente to taunt Kissinger on his policy for dealing with the Soviets in an exchange on May 9, 1975.

triangle." During the 1970s, they tried to play the United States against the Soviet Union both to reduce Moscow's military pressures against them and to caution Washington that it should not take China's fear of the Soviet Union for granted as a basis for U.S. foot-dragging on the normalization issue. PRC attacks on U.S. détente policy throughout the 1970s were designed to encourage Washington to confront the Soviets more forcefully, as this would make it more difficult for Moscow to direct its attention to China and would limit the possibilities for any coordinated U.S.-Soviet action against the PRC.

At the same time, Chinese leaders occasionally hinted at the prospect of some improvement in Sino-Soviet relations—both to worry Washington and to deflate Moscow's pressures on China. In October 1974, for example, on the eve of the Ford-Brezhnev summit meeting at Vladivostok, the Chinese leadership sent a telegram of congratulations to the Soviet Union on the anniversary of the Bolshevik revolution, proposing in the communication a nonaggression pact. Coming as it did amid tensions in the Sino-American relationship, the cable sparked off press speculation about possible amelioration of the Beijing-Moscow feud. Deng Xiaoping then proceeded to deflate the speculation in his meeting with Kissinger, who had just arrived in Beijing from Vladivostok, with a strong affirmation that in the Chinese view the Brezhnev policy of hegemony was unlikely to change.[60] A year later, speculation about an improvement in Sino-Soviet relations was again generated when the Chinese released the crew of a Soviet helicopter that had strayed into PRC territory, with the announcement that an investigation had shown the intrusions to have been accidental—this after months of PRC attacks on the Soviets for having used the intrusion as a purposeful provocation.[61]

A subsequent period of marked improvement in Sino-Soviet relations after Mao's death, in 1981–1982, coincided with a sharp deterioration in both U.S.-Soviet and U.S.-PRC relations. PRC

60. Deng-Kissinger, November 25–26, 1974.

61. The release of the helicopter crew may very well have been related to internal political maneuvering associated with the rise in influence of then–Public Security Chief Hua Guofeng. The exact dynamic of this particular incident remains unclear.

leaders apparently decided to seek to reduce the level of Sino-Soviet hostility both to deflate Soviet pressures against them and to avoid being caught in the middle of the deteriorating Soviet-American relationship. This shift in policy was also intended to build additional pressure on the United States to end its arms sales to Taiwan. The Chinese had become painfully aware that the high level of Sino-Soviet hostility of the Mao era was not only subjecting them to growing political and military pressures from Moscow, but also limiting their negotiating room for maneuver with the United States. Because they assumed the United States would take China for granted because of its presumed fear of the Soviets, and for other reasons as well, the Chinese attempted to reduce Sino-Soviet political tensions, even when Moscow's military buildup in Asia was continuing unabated.

To gain maximum negotiating advantage from the shift in policy toward the Soviet Union, PRC leaders gratuitously noted for U.S. officials the presumed concern of the American people about signs of improvement in Sino-Soviet relations and continued their assurances that the PRC would continue to struggle against Soviet hegemony.[62] When President Reagan visited Beijing in the spring of 1984, PRC leaders gratuitously called his attention to the imminent arrival of Soviet First Deputy Premier Ivan Arkipov, putting the United States on notice that the PRC was not without alternatives if the U.S.-PRC relationship did not continue to improve.[63]

As noted earlier, this compulsion to play on political rivalries as part of the political (and commercial) negotiating process seems rooted in the highly factionalized quality of Chinese politics.

Beat Up on One's Friends

Another notable Chinese negotiating tactic is focusing pressures on "old friends." Inasmuch as the Chinese devote such effort in the early phases of a negotiation to identifying sympathetic

62. See, for example, Foreign Minister Wu Xueqian's use of this ploy with Secretary of State George Shultz on February 3, 1983.

63. They also sought to contrast the problem areas in the U.S.-PRC relationship with the close ties between China and Japan, which, it was asserted, would endure into the twenty-first century. See Zhao-Reagan, April 27, 1984; Li Xiannien-Reagan, April 27, 1984; and Hu Yaobang-Reagan, April 27, 1984..

interlocutors and working to establish *guanxi* with them, it is logical enough that in the later, formal phases they seek to pressure those who have demonstrated interest in or commitment to the relationship.

This pattern was evident in the pressures they applied on Henry Kissinger in the fall of 1975 to move him to complete the normalization process. Because Kissinger had established his political reputation both nationally and internationally on his role in building the U.S.-PRC relationship, Chinese leaders assumed that for reasons of "face," as well as his desire to have a positive relationship with China as a major component of his policy for dealing with the Soviets, Kissinger was vulnerable to threats of a "bad" presidential visit in late 1975. Thus, they created the expectation of a substanceless visit by President Ford if significant progress was not made toward establishing U.S.-PRC diplomatic relations (and thus fulfilling President Nixon's expressed intention of completing the normalization process in his second term). In the last eighteen months of Kissinger's tenure as secretary of state, PRC dealings with him bordered at times on the contemptuous, as he was in their view a friend who had failed to fulfill a commitment.[64]

Another example of pressuring old friends is the treatment given vice presidential candidate George Bush in August 1980, when he was dispatched by presidential candidate Reagan to Beijing to explain the Reagan position on China policy. Deng Xiaoping and other senior officials warned Bush that if the Republican party platform and Reagan's campaign statements about the intention to restore official relations with Taiwan were implemented, there would be a "regression" in U.S.-PRC relations. After Bush departed Beijing, PRC officials conveyed to American journalists in the Chinese capital the opinion that Bush's mission on behalf of candidate Reagan had been a "failure," as

64. This is evident in Deng's challenging of Kissinger's motives and the veracity of some of his statements to the Chinese. See, for example, Deng's comments to a congressional delegation on September 5, 1974; his inquiry to Senator Mansfield on December 10, 1974, about whether Kissinger had "fully briefed PRC leaders after the Vladivostok summit"; and the haughty tone of Qiao Guanhua in his exchanges with Kissinger on October 28, 1975, and October 8, 1976.

it had not resolved PRC concerns about the Republican party's China policy.

So harsh was Deng's treatment of his old friend Bush that when the vice president was again dispatched to Beijing in May 1982 to help resolve continuing differences over the arms-sales issue, Deng conceded almost apologetically that his "candid" presentation of August 1980 may have offended the vice president, "but it was necessary for us to frankly state our views."[65] All the same, the Chinese continued to keep pressure on Bush throughout his first term as vice president by expressing their expectation that he would fulfill his obligations to the relationship as a "friend of China." In a letter to Bush from Premier Zhao Ziyang, just after the inauguration, the premier expressed hope that "in view of the part you played in promoting the normalization of Sino-U.S. relations and your understanding of China, you will . . . make significant contributions to the further development of our relations."[66] And on the eve of Bush's May 1982 visit to the PRC, Chinese officials warned their counterparts in the U.S. embassy in Beijing that the vice president's trip would be a failure if he came unprepared to resolve the Taiwan arms-sales issue.[67]

This Chinese practice of pressuring their friends is all the more noticeable in view of their evident lack of skill in lobbying American officials who are either skeptical of or hostile to China and to the U.S.-PRC relationship. The Chinese seem to feel comfortable only in dealing with those who share a basic inclination to establish positive *guanxi* at the human level. Yet these same friends are the ones who receive the brunt of the pressure when there are problems to be resolved, for the Chinese assume—not without reason—that those who see value in the U.S.-PRC relationship are the ones who will work to resolve the problems and thereby sustain their status as friends of China.

---

65. Deng-Bush, May 8, 1982.

66. Zhao-Bush letter, January 20, 1981.

67. Zhu Qizhen-Freeman, May 20, 1982.

"Your Chinese Friends Are in Trouble"

A negotiating ploy that mirrors the pressuring of old friends is the warning to foreign officials that if they do not meet certain Chinese political needs, their "old friends" in the PRC system will lose their influence—thus cutting off the foreign government from political access, or at least weakening the influence of officials friendly to it.

This ploy was first evident in the U.S.-PRC relationship in late 1971, when officials of the PRC embassy in London let American contacts know that if President Nixon did not give Premier Zhou Enlai anything on the normalization issue during his trip to Beijing, Zhou would be vulnerable to attacks from his opponents in the leadership. The most blatant use of the tactic was during the negotiations of 1981–1982 on U.S. arms sales to Taiwan, when Deng Xiaoping repeatedly told U.S. officials and former officials, "Should the Chinese government and leadership fail to handle the Taiwan question in a correct manner, they would forfeit the support of the entire Chinese people."[68] A few months later, he told Vice President Mondale, "If on this question the leaders go against the will of the people, then at least we should step down from our posts."[69]

Was Deng's warning a hollow threat? It is hard for an outside observer to reach a firm judgment; foreign officials generally know so little about the balance of forces within the senior PRC leadership that they are unable to estimate the impact of their policies on the Chinese political process. Outside analysts can make commonsense judgments about the significance of certain issues within the PRC political system, but ultimately, foreign governments will set their policies according to considerations of their own national interests, with the welfare of their friends in the Chinese government at best a marginal consideration.

---

68. Deng-Haig, June 16, 1981.

69. Deng-Mondale, November 22, 1981. See similar comments to former Secretary of Defense Harold Brown on October 18, 1981; former President Ford on March 26, 1981; and United Front official Liao Chengzhi to a U.S. citizen on July 14, 1982.

Nonetheless, Chinese officials will occasionally invoke the political vulnerabilities of their senior leaders to caution a foreign government, much as American negotiators cite the prospect of congressional opposition as the rationale for rejecting certain negotiating positions.

Threats ("Killing the Chicken to Warn the Monkey")

Prior to the establishment of U.S.-PRC diplomatic relations in 1979, threats did not constitute a prominent aspect of the normalization dialogue. Upon occasion there were oblique hints of some costly outcome of a failure to make progress, such as when Chairman Mao, in his first meeting with President Nixon, hinted at the awkward consequences for the president of a lack of progress toward normalization on his visit to the PRC.[70] But for the most part, during the years the Chinese were trying to draw the United States into a fully normalized relationship, they avoided the invocation of overt threats. Rather, they tended to hold back on active cooperation—to withhold the presumed benefits of an active relationship—rather than cite the dire consequences of some U.S. failure to accommodate to their position.

This style of negotiating changed significantly, however, after the completion of normalization in late 1978, as the relationship entered a phase of reaching concrete agreements. When PRC leaders decided in 1981 to press the United States to curtail its arms sales to Taiwan, overt threats became a major aspect of the negotiating process.

What conclusion can be drawn from this experience? It is evident that in at least several instances the Chinese changed negotiating positions and retreated from their threatened sanctions. At other times, however, they made good on their threats. They obviously go through a cost-benefit assessment of when realization of a threat, as opposed to a shift in position, will best serve

---

70. Said Mao to Nixon: "It is alright to talk well [in your forthcoming discussions with Premier Zhou] and also alright if there are no agreements, because what use is there if we stand in deadlock? Why is it that we must be able to reach results? . . . If we fail the first time, then people will ask why are we not able to succeed the first time? The only reason would be that we have taken the wrong road. What will they say if we succeed the second time?" (Mao-Nixon, February 21, 1972)

their interests. A U.S. negotiator should thus *not* assume that threats will invariably be carried out if PRC terms are not met.

At the same time, it would be wrong to assume that all Chinese threats are bluffs. PRC negotiators seem to place special emphasis on the credibility of their word. As Zhou Enlai sought to impress on Henry Kissinger during their early exchanges, "Our word counts" (Kissinger, 1979, p. 1056). How do Chinese negotiators seek to ensure the credibility of their threats? A number of the former American officials interviewed for this study opined that the Chinese seem to make minimal use of bluffing, to sustain the credibility of the threats they *do* invoke. They also use a technique for making threats credible that is called—to use their own vernacular—"killing the chicken to warn the monkey" *(sha-ji jing-hou),* i.e., taking some limited-cost action that validates their willingness to carry out a more substantial threat.

Formal Protests

In the pre-normalization period of U.S.-PRC confrontation, PRC officials established a clear and enduring record of asserting their position on certain issues (and documenting the wrongdoings of the United States) through formal protests. This was most evident in the more than 497 "serious protests" registered with the U.S. government in the 1950s and 1960s (through the ambassadorial talks at Warsaw) for alleged American violations of PRC territory and airspace, primarily associated with U.S. military operations near the PRC-claimed Paracel Islands in the South China Sea during the Vietnam War.

A similar pattern of protests began again in 1980, when the Carter administration resumed sales of military equipment to Taiwan, and continued into the Reagan administration in response to media reports that the U.S. government was considering sales of an advanced fighter aircraft to Taiwan. After issuance of the joint U.S.-PRC communiqué on the arms-sales issue on August 17, 1982, PRC officials registered formal protests in response to each new announcement of an American arms transaction with the island.

While PRC officials probably have no expectation that such protests will bring about an immediate change in U.S. behavior, they believe that the constant stating of their position establishes a record that can be invoked at some later date. They probably also assume that the protests will build some pressure on the U.S. government to abide by the "principles" of the relationship and the terms of the August agreement, thus constraining U.S. action while building the record of U.S. wrongdoings.

Escalation of Demands

Another approach the Chinese have used to build pressure on American negotiators, even as they were attempting to draw the United States into a more active relationship, is the escalation of demands—especially regarding the Taiwan issue. We have documented the initial exchanges with the Nixon administration in which PRC leaders enticingly hinted that "it would be necessary to create the conditions" to resolve the Taiwan issue. They subsequently indicated in 1971 that they expected the United States to withdraw all its troops from Taiwan. When direct, high-level U.S.-PRC contacts were established in the summer of 1971, Zhou Enlai pressed the United States to recognize the PRC as the "sole legitimate government" of China and to acknowledge Taiwan's status as an inalienable part of China, as a basis for establishing diplomatic relations.

This tactic puts the adversary government off balance by setting an agenda to which it must react, while the Chinese put themselves in a position where any modifications of their own initially stated terms can be characterized as making concessions or showing flexibility.

Provocation

In addition to using provocations to facilitate the development of the U.S.-PRC normalization dialogue and to advance China's maneuverability within the strategic triangle, the Chinese also used them to build pressures on American negotiators, to get them to reassess their policy positions relative to the PRC, and to force them to take a stand on issues considered important by the Chinese.

The clearest example of this tactic occurred in the spring of 1975, when the Gang of Four was increasingly assertive within the PRC leadership and the influence of the hospitalized Zhou Enlai and the aging Mao Zedong was weakening. In late March, the Chinese informed the National Committee on U.S.-China Relations, which manages cultural exchanges with the PRC, that a performing arts group scheduled to tour the United States in April had in its repertoire a song entitled, "People of Taiwan, Our Brothers." The song contained the line, "We are determined to liberate Taiwan and let the light of the sun shine on the island," which was viewed in Washington as highly provocative in the U.S. domestic political context.

A series of exchanges between the U.S. Department of State and the PRC Liaison Office led to a U.S. demand that the offensive song be deleted from the repertoire; otherwise, the group's tour would be "postponed." In reply, the Chinese asserted that U.S. objections to the song demonstrated that the Ford administration was not sincere in its commitment to the principles of the Shanghai Communiqué (which held that Taiwan's future was a domestic issue for the Chinese to resolve themselves) and that since this was an issue of principle, the Chinese government could never yield to foreign pressure on the matter.[71] Despite U.S. efforts to suggest a way out of the impasse, the Chinese held firm and the cultural group's tour was finally canceled.

What was Beijing's purpose in pressing the United States to accept such a provocative cultural performance? One interpretation at the time was that the Chinese wanted to sensitize the Ford administration to the seriousness of their concern with the Taiwan issue, and to do so well in advance of the president's fall trip to Beijing. A second interpretation (which in hindsight seems more credible) is that "liberals" in the PRC leadership wanted to embarrass the Zhou-Deng moderates for their America policy, and they used the provocation to demonstrate either that the United States would resist action on the Taiwan issue or, if the administration acceded to the touring group's song, that political repercussions in Taipei and Washington would induce added strains in the U.S.-Taiwan relationship.

71. Habib-Han Xu exchanges of March 19, March 20, March 23, and March 25, 1975.

Whichever interpretation is correct, this incident is but one example of the use of political provocations to apply pressure on an adversary government in order to induce policy changes. It also seems a clear case in which internal political factionalism in Beijing induced a provocative foreign-policy initiative.

Loss of Control

We noted at the outset of this analysis that Chinese officials will go to great lengths to conduct negotiations on their own territory, to maximize their ability to control the ambience and to establish the *guanxi* that is at the core of their efforts to influence a foreign government's negotiating position. But such control can also be used to raise pressures on a foreign negotiating team. After the Chinese have impressed visiting foreign officials with their capacity for seemingly effortless and unerring control over the protocol of a visit, subsequent delays of meetings or apparent uncertainty in the management of a visit become all the more unnerving, for the visitors assume that even an inadvertent lapse is purposeful and designed to convey some subtle political message.

Henry Kissinger summarized this sense of unease in describing his reaction to the unexplained cancellation of a communiqué-drafting session during the last day of his secret visit to Beijing in July, 1971:

> *[Zhou Enlai] designated Huang Hua as his representative for drafting the announcement, and then left. But Huang Hua did not show up right away. The inexplicable waiting was all the more ominous because we were talking not about an elaborate communiqué but about a statement of a paragraph or two announcing a Presidential visit to Peking. We never found out whether it was a deliberate tactic to unsettle us, whether there was a Politburo meeting, whether Mao insisted on reviewing the talks, or whether, as was most likely, we faced a combination of all of these. Finally, Huang Hua showed up without a word of explanation, urbane, affable, imperturbable. (Kissinger, 1979, p. 751)*

Less ambiguous examples of purposeful PRC management of negotiations to create a sense of disorientation and loss of control are the previously noted occasions when Presidents Nixon and Ford were kept in the dark about the scheduling of sessions with Chairman Mao, only to be surprised with awkwardly timed encounters, and the purposeful stalling in October 1975 designed to undercut Kissinger's effort to negotiate a draft communiqué in advance of the Ford visit. A clear example of how Zhou Enlai used the timing of meals to control the mood of substantive exchanges, and even to cut off a Kissinger rebuttal of his own critique of U.S. policy, is described in this episode from the July 1971 secret visit to Beijing:

> *The mood [in the second session] was very different from that of the previous evening. With very few preliminaries Chou [Zhou] launched into a forceful presentation of the Chinese point of view. With little rhetorical flourish Chou put forward much of what I came later to know as Chinese Communist liturgy—that there was "much turmoil under the heavens"; that Taiwan was part of China; that China supported the "just struggle" of the North Vietnamese; that the big powers were colluding against China. . . . I then launched into a deliberately brusk point-by-point rebuttal of Chou's presentation. Chou stopped me after the first point, saying the duck would get cold if we did not eat first. At lunch over Peking duck the mood changed and Chou's geniality returned. (Kissinger, 1979, p. 750)*

On his subsequent visit to Beijing in October 1971, when negotiation of the first drafts of the Shanghai Communiqué began, Kissinger was subjected for the first time to Chinese use of fatigue to put a foreign negotiator under physical as well as psychological pressure:

> *After stuffing us with roast duck, Chou submitted his [communiqué draft] in the evening. It was unprecedented in design. It stated the Chinese position on a whole host of issues in extremely uncompromising terms. It left blank pages for our position, which was assumed to be contrary.*
>
> . . .
>
> *After a brief break I told Chou that I would accept his basic approach. The communiqué could contain an extended statement of differences; we would supply the American position for those areas later. However, the language of the disagreements had to be compatible with the occasion [of a presidential visit] . . . there would have to be some common positions, or else the whole [Nixon] journey would be seen as an exercise in futility. I promised to submit a counterdraft the next morning.*
>
> *It [the drafting] turned into a contest of physical endurance. Lord redrafted the communiqué while I got three hours of sleep. Then he went to bed and I reworked his draft for the remainder of the night.*

> *Our counterdraft of October 25 ushered in a session that lasted the whole day, interrupted for several hours while the Chinese translated our text, studied it, and, no doubt, cleared their position with Mao. (Kissinger, 1979, pp. 782–783)*

These recollections illustrate the PRC use of unpredictability in scheduling negotiating sessions, inconvenient timing of exchanges (late at night after heavy meals), and the general dislocation of having to negotiate in an unfamiliar environment to induce in the visiting official a sense of disorientation, fatigue, and loss of control.

"Bad Guy–Good Guy"

A universal negotiating ploy that is also evident in PRC diplomatic practice is the alternation of pressures and accommodating exchanges, often by including both "hard" and "soft" officials in the formal meetings. This tactic was evident to diplomats who dealt with Qing dynasty officials in the nineteenth century (Eastman, 1967; Fairbank and Teng, 1961), and it is a pattern that recurred in the normalization exchanges. Zhou Enlai, for the most part, made his presentations in understated and urbane fashion, but periodically he would launch into sharp attacks on the American position, evidently under instruction from Mao Zedong, who remained a largely unseen but contentious orchestrator of the negotiations from "behind the curtains" *(mu-hou).*

This "bad guy–good guy" pattern appears in the contrasting styles of former Foreign Minister Huang Hua and Deng Xiaoping, who from 1978 to 1982 functioned as a team. Huang's presentational style was self-righteously acerbic, unyielding, and demanding, and he would tend to drag out exchanges until the positions of the two sides deadlocked. Deng, in contrast, would present himself (usually at the conclusion of a series of exchanges) as low-key, rational, and concerned with finding a common basis for agreement.

There is no doubt a strong element of role-playing as well as responsiveness to internal political guidance in this pattern, for Deng at times could also be quite acerbic and taunting in his presentations; in contrast, Huang—who was at his most vicious in the exchanges at Panmunjom in 1953, when the Chinese were determined to force a break in the negotiations with the United States (Dean, 1966)—so impressed Kissinger with his "wise, practical," and accommodating negotiating style that he was characterized by Kissinger after their first year of encounters as "my new friend" (Kissinger, 1979, pp. 752, 774).

Split the Politician from His Advisers

One Chinese tactic frequently noted in commercial negotiations is that of separating a senior negotiator from his staff of specialized advisers when decisions are to be made. Chinese escorts will arrange sightseeing trips for businessmen and then unexpectedly convene a decisionmaking discussion in a limousine when the chief of the negotiating team is alone with his PRC counterpart and a Chinese interpreter. PRC commercial negotiators also privately debunk the expertise of foreign advisory personnel in discussions with senior negotiators in an effort to undermine the confidence placed in them.

Similarly, in political negotiations, expert staff are often separated from the official they are accompanying, for example, at banquets (ostensibly for reasons of protocol). The senior official is then given information or urged to state opinions beyond the earshot of staff who could either record the exchanges for later reference or caution him in his responses.

The most blatant PRC use of this tactic in dealings with the United States occurred in 1977–1978 following Secretary of State Vance's August visit to Beijing (in which Vance had presented the Carter administration's initial approach to completing the normalization process). The Chinese must have concluded that Vance's lawyerly approach to the issue and his perceived reluctance to take a strong stand against the Soviet Union made him an unpromising negotiating counterpart, for not long thereafter senior PRC officials began sending the message to President Carter that "Sino-American relations are not a diplomatic question but a political question [and] it is necessary to consider this question [of normalization] from the viewpoint of long-term strategic interests."[72] This was an oblique way of saying that they hoped

72. Vance-Huang Hua, September 28, 1977.

the president would manage the normalization issue from the White House rather than allowing it to be handled by Secretary Vance and his colleagues in the State Department. A few months later, their preferences were partially accommodated, when National Security Adviser Brzezinski presented himself to the Chinese as an interlocutor on strategic issues.

"You Are Hurting the Feelings of a Billion Chinese" (The Pressure of Mass Opinion)

Chinese decisionmakers have impressed most official American interlocutors as being coldly calculating in their approach to negotiations. Emotional public reaction to their efforts—given the elitist, Marxist-Leninist structure of the PRC political system and China's long tradition of authoritarian government—has not been a significant theme in their presentations to U.S. counterparts. Moreover, it is not clear to outside analysts exactly how the PRC leadership assesses public support for its policies or how the opinions of the masses play on the leadership, although as politicians they cannot be unmindful of matters of public support.

In the post-Mao years of negotiating contact with the PRC, American officials began to hear Chinese leaders invoke the issue of public reaction to their policies as a way of pressing the United States to accommodate to their views.

Deng Xiaoping claimed that public opinion and the purported resentments of his billion countrymen on matters related to Taiwan were serious constraints on his negotiating flexibility. Was this merely a rhetorical device for obtaining American acquiescence to his position? To some degree, but probably not entirely. Unlike Mao's imperial style of leadership, Deng's restructuring of China's political and economic system gave at least a limited and constrained voice to public opinion—as at Democracy Wall or in the reconstitution of the National People's Congress. Thus, even though U.S. decisionmakers must quite properly formulate China policy on the basis of American national interests and not considerations of China's domestic politics, Deng no doubt includes in some incalculable way "the feelings of a billion Chinese" in *his* policy calculations.

Press Play

The Chinese Communists discovered early in their history that the press could be a potent weapon in their struggle against their Nationalist (Kuomintang) enemies. Not only was the mass media, in the Bolshevik tradition, seen as a basic tool of "agitprop"—of mobilizing the masses in support of party policies—it was also an essential element of a negotiating context in which the party had to compete with the Nationalist government both on the battlefield and in the fight for domestic and international support. As Mao commented in his 1945 article "On the Chungking Negotiations," a major reason the Communist Party had entered into "peace" talks with Chiang Kai-shek was to "explode the rumor spread by the Kuomintang that the Communist Party did not want peace and unity." He went on to describe how negotiating positions were formulated as much for their impact on public opinion as out of any expectation of reaching agreement with the Nationalists:

> *All the means of propaganda in China, except the Hsinhua News Agency, are now controlled by the Kuomintang. They are all rumor factories. Concerning the current negotiations, they have spread the rumor that the Communist Party just wants territory and will make no concessions. . . . Subject to the principle of not damaging the fundamental interests of the people, it is permissible to make certain concessions. . . . By conceding areas in the south, we have completely exploded the Kuomintang's rumors before the people of all China and the whole world. (Mao Zedong, 1965, p. 57)*

During the 1950s and 1960s, in its dealings with the United States, Beijing used the international press to justify positions that could not be resolved behind closed doors (Young, 1968, pp. 111–112 and passim); in contrast, in the normalization negotiations, the Chinese used the mass media to help build public support for a U.S.-PRC relationship—and to pressure the United States to accede to negotiating positions favorable to PRC interests.

From Henry Kissinger's first encounter with PRC leaders, Zhou Enlai used the press as a counterpoint to the private negotiations. While Kissinger was secretly flying to Beijing from Pakistan in July 1971, *New York Times* correspondent James Reston was journeying to the Chinese capital by train as a public guest of the premier (Kissinger, 1979, pp. 753–754). Zhou's lengthy interview with Reston, published on August 10 (less than a month after the public announcement of Kissinger's secret trip and the Nixon presidential visit), enabled the PRC leadership to get into public view its positions on the full range of bilateral and international issues covered in the private official talks with Kissinger—and it provided a public channel that could be played against the Nixon administration if the official discussions proved unpromising.

It soon became clear that Zhou's experience with mass media was still limited to newspapers and books, that he did not yet fully appreciate the potential of the "new" medium of television. In his first discussion with Kissinger about the mechanics of the Nixon visit, Zhou estimated that the president would want to bring along a press entourage of not more than ten! The final number agreed to by the Chinese, after considerable discussion, was over 250, including TV commentators and technicians. Zhou was well aware, however, that unlike the Americans, he did not have to defend his policies before an inquisitive press. As he remarked to Kissinger in the context of a critique of the U.S. government's position on Chinese representation in the United Nations:

> *There is also the question of world public opinion [in reacting to U.S. government policy]. It's easier for us here, because we don't have to hold a press conference every week and can wait maybe half a year before giving our answer. Although perhaps now the situation may change.*[73]

The premier's closing premonition that "now the situation may change" may not have been more than his private anticipation of the imminent arrival in Beijing of *New York Times* correspondent Reston; but Zhou and other PRC leaders were quick to grasp the possibilities of television. They responded to Kissinger's descriptions of how the Nixon administration intended to use the print and electronic media to give outreach to its China initiative by not only agreeing to an enormous presidential press entourage, but rapidly constructing two earth stations for

73. Zhou-Kissinger, July 10, 1971.

receiving and transmitting satellite television transmissions so that the presidential visit—the official banquets, the tours of historic sites, and the issuance of the Shanghai Communiqué—could project China and its new foreign policy to a global audience.

How have PRC officials used the mass media as a component of their approach to negotiations—and especially as a way of bringing pressure to bear on their U.S. counterparts? The record suggests the following tactical uses of the media as an adjunct to the negotiating process.

"Pump Priming" (Setting a Discussion Agenda)

The Chinese have skillfully used the press in advance of official negotiating encounters to publicly set a discussion agenda. Mao Zedong's interview with Edgar Snow in late 1970 (published in *Life* magazine in April of the following year, just after "ping-pong diplomacy" had raised public expectations about a possible thaw in the U.S.-PRC confrontation) and Zhou Enlai's interview with James Reston helped to set the stage at the outset of the official exchanges between the Chinese leaders and the Nixon administration. Other interesting examples of this technique are Deng Xiaoping's interview with a congressional delegation headed by Senator Sam Nunn of Georgia three weeks in advance of his official visit to Washington. In the interview, Deng made public the contents of the Third Plenum decisions regarding peaceful reunification with Taiwan, defusing pressures on the Taiwan issue that would likely come from his forthcoming meetings with other congressional leaders in Washington. Deng also gave an interview to *Time* magazine just before his trip to Washington, publicly setting out his perspectives on a wide range of issues to which the American side had to react. As President Carter said to Deng in their first formal discussion, "I have read your statement [on world issues] that was published in *Time* magazine, and I thought you might be interested in hearing about our policies."[74]

A similar approach was used in 1981, just before the Chinese pressed the Reagan administration to negotiate on the issue of

74. Carter-Deng, January 29, 1979.

U.S. arms sales to Taiwan. On September 30, PRC media carried Marshal Ye Jianying's nine-point program for peaceful reunification with Taiwan. Two days later, Ambassador Chai Zemin called on National Security Adviser Richard Allen to inquire if he had read the Ye program.

The Trap of Public Visibility

Chinese leaders became quite conscious during the early 1970s of the way in which the intense media attention to Kissinger's periodic visits to Beijing tended to trap the Nixon and Ford administrations in the high expectations raised by the normalization dialogue. Given the limited "hard" information that was made available to the press about the substantive content of the talks and the degree to which even the mood of the discussions affected the China factor in Kissinger's approach to dealing with the Soviet Union, Chinese leaders felt that their ability to shape press perceptions of the state of the U.S.-PRC relationship gave them significant leverage. In late 1974, for example, PRC officials began to "background" the resident American press in Beijing about various "problems" in their dealings with Washington, thus stimulating stories about a cooling in the relationship. Deng, in his initial meeting with Kissinger in November 1974, debunked rumors about a chilling of the relationship;[75] but at the first formal negotiating session, with the large traveling press contingent in the room for a photo opportunity, Deng needled Kissinger about the state of the relationship —to the delight of the newsmen:

> Deng: *It probably would be good if one day we would be able to exchange views in Washington.*
>
> Kissinger: *I hope we can do that very soon, [but] your Foreign Minister always refuses my invitations.*
>
> Deng: *It is difficult for him to come now. What will he do if he meets the Chiang Kai-shek Ambassador to Washington?*
>
> *[The press contingent is escorted from the room.]*
>
> Kissinger: . . . *we are prepared on this visit to discuss the whole question of normalization.*

75. Deng-Kissinger, November 25, 1974.

Deng: *That is good.*[76]

Deng seemed to take particular delight in priming the press in such opening mood-setting exchanges—usually putting Kissinger on the defensive. But he could also use this technique to deflate pressures on the visiting American delegation, as when he congratulated President Ford, during Ford's December 1975 visit to Beijing, for his "successful" discussion with Chairman Mao, noting that the two sides had "set a new style" in the relationship by not being compelled to issue a formal communiqué.[77] (In thus giving the president some "face" during his visit, and by defusing the issue of the lack of a formal communiqué, Deng was of course trying to put the president in his debt while also maintaining a public atmosphere conducive to PRC efforts to sustain the U.S.-PRC relationship.)

PRC officials' awareness of the value of public visibility in their negotiating encounters was revealed in the fall of 1981 when Foreign Minister Huang Hua, having pressed a series of demands on the Reagan administration, concluded his meetings in Washington with an effort to get into the public record the fact that the administration had agreed to hold discussions on the arms-sales issue. Secretary of State Haig sought to diffuse the impression that negotiations on the arms-sales issue were under way; but in a meeting with the press after their final session, Huang made it clear that the issue was under discussion, a fact that PRC media were quick to play up.[78]

Public Attack

In general, PRC officials have been loath to attack U.S. officials publicly and by name; such overt criticism, in their political culture, is reserved for adversaries. In the normalization period,

76. Deng-Kissinger, November 26, 1974.

77. Deng-Ford, December 3, 1975.

78. See Haig-Huang Hua, October 30, 1981; also the *Xinhua* dispatch from Washington of the same date reporting Huang's comment that "the two sides had discussed the question of U.S. arms sales to Taiwan. The date, venue, and level of further talks between the two sides would be decided by the two sides through consultations." Haig had merely told the press—as had been privately agreed—"the two sides had discussed current major international problems and bilateral relations including the Taiwan question."

their objective was to move the U.S. government to take positions favorable to PRC interests, not to destroy the growing relationship. Thus, their public criticisms of American officials were muted and mostly by indirection rather than by direct attack. This was the case in 1974 when they wanted to put pressure on Henry Kissinger for his détente approach to dealing with the Soviet Union. Rather than criticize Kissinger by name, they took advantage of public disclosure of a purported speech by one of Kissinger's close associates, Helmut Sonnenfeldt, on U.S./European policy to publicly attack the "Sonnenfeldt Doctrine," which, said PRC media, demonstrated that the United States was accommodating Soviet hegemony over Europe.[79] The press criticism was a thinly veiled attack on Kissinger, in the traditional Chinese pattern of "pointing at the mulberry to curse the locust" *(zhi sang ma huai).*

PRC officials occasionally use direct public attack to establish a limit on an adversary's negotiating position. Through public criticism they try to establish their opposition to a given policy, creating a situation in which their negotiating counterpart will assume that since the PRC has gone public with a position it will be most reluctant to lose face or credibility by changing policy. Such was the case in the fall of 1977, following Secretary of State Vance's visit to Beijing. Unauthorized rumors in the American press—which the Chinese probably assumed had official inspiration—hinted that Deng had shown "flexibility" on normalization issues in his private discussions with Vance. Deng, anxious to protect himself against domestic critics as well as to undercut any impression that he would accommodate Vance's concern for an official American presence on Taiwan after normalization, publicly criticized the secretary's negotiating position in a meeting with a group of American newspaper editors, characterizing his discussions with Vance as a "step backward" in the normalization dialogue.[80]

---

79. See *Xinhua* attacks on the "Sonnenfeldt Doctrine" of April 19 and April 21, 1976.

80. *The New York Times,* September 7, 1977.

Raising Expectations

Given the demonstrated effectiveness of using the mass media to generate public pressures on the U.S. government, the Chinese have tried—with varying degrees of success—to control the level of visibility of issues when they believed public expectations would work to their advantage in the negotiating process. During the second half of 1978, when the final phase of normalization exchanges was under way (and when, at U.S. request, the fact of the negotiations was to be kept confidential), PRC officials could barely constrain their impulse to let it be known that the normalization process was in a final phase. In late July, the U.S. Liaison Office in Beijing protested to the Foreign Ministry a Chinese indiscretion to the French about the first Woodcock-Huang sessions on the normalization issue.[81] And on November 18, Deng, in a meeting with a Japanese Komeito party delegation, opined in public that he thought it would take only "two seconds" to complete the normalization of U.S.-PRC relations. Deng also expressed his personal interest in visiting the United States.

While the Chinese did abide by the Carter administration's request that the existence of the talks remain confidential—a request made by the U.S. side precisely to minimize the kind of public pressures that had constrained Kissinger—their instinct was to raise public expectations about the negotiation and thus subject the U.S. government to the pressures of domestic and international opinion.

A similar example occurred in 1977, when PRC officials told David Rockefeller that it would be easy to resolve the languishing private-claims/blocked-assets issue, thus stimulating considerable private-sector and press commentary. When governmental exchanges on the topic were resumed, however, it became clear at an official level that the Chinese were not prepared to soften their negotiating position or to accommodate U.S. legal requirements in order to consummate an agreement. The issue continued to drift until the spring of 1979, when the Chinese, in the first major effort to implement Deng's economic modernization

81. Lin-Roy, July 25, 1978.

program, finally compromised sufficiently to reach agreement with the Carter administration.

Provocation

The Chinese use of political provocations to influence a negotiation is a counterpart to their use of the press. It is likely that Beijing anticipated in the mid-1970s that occasional moderating gestures toward the Soviet Union would elicit lively press speculation in the United States about the possibility of a Sino-Soviet reconciliation; and even if the Chinese didn't hold such expectations, the evident reactions that *did* occur clearly demonstrated to them a capacity to evoke a public response that would work to their advantage.

PRC media upon occasion have attacked U.S. policies in a way that suggests they anticipate that public criticism may provoke a change in a position they consider objectionable or move the U.S. government to take some desired action. For example, in the spring of 1975, not long after the collapse of the Thieu government in South Vietnam, PRC media carried an article characterizing the United States as "strategically passive"—a theme that the Chinese knew, from official exchanges, was likely to elicit a sharp reaction from Secretary of State Kissinger. The secretary was concerned that the Soviets, North Koreans, or other adversaries of the United States would take advantage of the mood of the time to press their own interests much more aggressively. Kissinger did, in fact, protest the characterization of strategic passivity in a discussion with Liaison Office Chief Huang Zhen on May 9; and the Chinese criticism was probably one of the factors that moved the United States to take military action a few days later against the new Cambodian Communist government in the *Mayaguez* affair.

Public attacks by the PRC on alleged Western appeasement of the Soviet Union in the latter half of the 1970s parallel private Chinese demarches on the same subject to officials of the Ford and Carter administrations.[82] It may be assumed that such criticism was intended to provoke a more confrontational U.S. policy

82. See, for example, Kissinger-Qiao Guanhua, September 28, 1975; Huang Hua-Vance, August 24, 1977; Huang Hua-Brzezinski, May 20, 1978.

toward the Soviet Union—which would divert Soviet pressures away from the PRC.[83]

Limit-Setting

Chinese press commentary paralleling a negotiation often seems intended to establish a perception in the minds of the foreign negotiators of the limits to PRC flexibility on the issue under discussion. By making a position public, the Chinese may assume that they are "loading" the thinking of their counterpart government officials with their preferred position, as well as convincing them that, having gone public with a firm statement, they are unlikely—for reasons of credibility or face—to show flexibility at the bargaining table. Thus, after 1974, PRC media stressed that normalization could be realized only on the basis of the Japan formula; and in early 1982, a *People's Daily* commentary asserted that there had to be a time limit on U.S. arms sales to Taiwan.

The Chinese are highly conscious of the differing levels of authoritativeness of their various media. In internal documents, they clearly distinguish between the PRC-controlled Hong Kong press (the *Da Gong Bao* and *Xin Wan Bao*), the unofficial mainland media such as the *Wen Hui Bao* and the *Guang Ming Ri Bao,* the governmental news outlet *Xinhua She,* and authoritative political media, especially *Ren Min Ri Bao (People's Daily)*. They will often present positions on topics under negotiation in a much "harder" tone in unofficial media in order to influence the expectations of their foreign counterparts about the limits of their flexibility, while retaining the option of modifying such positions, since they were not made in an official publication.

Enticement

During the arms-sales negotiation of 1982, the Chinese first floated a hint of compromise on the issue of a time limit on

83. Chinese pressures on the United States to be more aggressive in dealing with the Soviets are a mirror image of PRC efforts in the late 1950s and early 1960s to get Moscow to abandon détente with Washington and adopt a more "revolutionary" foreign policy. These Chinese pressures, which were seen by the Khrushchev leadership as provocative and adventurist, were no doubt intended to minimize the possibility of a détente in U.S.-Soviet relations—which would have isolated the PRC and created the threat of Moscow-Washington "collusion" against Chinese interests. The Chinese, thus, have attempted to provoke *both* the United States and Soviets to confront each other, to the presumed benefit of PRC security.

U.S. sales in a *Xinhua* commentary. Indeed, on March 2, as a new round of negotiations was beginning, a Foreign Ministry official explicitly—and privately—called the attention of U.S. embassy personnel to what he characterized as flexibility on the time limit issue in the just-published press commentary.[84]

What was the purpose of floating a hint of compromise in a public medium? It may be that the Chinese, in characteristic projective-test fashion, were hoping to stimulate the United States to respond with a new negotiating position that would be more forthcoming in meeting their objectives. The vague wording of the *Xinhua* commentary did not formally commit the PRC to a more flexible position, yet it might entice the United States to come forth with a specific reaction to which the Chinese would have the flexibility of responding at their own initiative.

Feedback

It is worth noting that Chinese officials, since the onset of the normalization dialogue, revealed a timely access to virtually all American mass media; and PRC management of the negotiating process has shown considerable sensitivity to the effects of press statements by U.S. administration officials and congressmen, and even of totally private press commentary.

During the Nixon presidential visit of 1972, Zhou Enlai disclosed to Secretary of State William Rogers that Mao had first seen signs of change in U.S. China policy in Nixon's *Foreign Affairs* article (Nixon, 1967), which (even during the height of the Cultural Revolution) had been translated and circulated in the internal publication *Reference Materials (Cankao Ziliao)*. When Kissinger arrived in Beijing in July 1971, during a round-the-world trip, Zhou quoted to him from a speech Nixon had delivered in Kansas City a few days before. Kissinger was nonplussed because he had not seen the speech himself (or known of its existence); nor had he received a copy from U.S. embassies along his travel route. Yet the PRC premier had this latest presidential statement —which he loaned to Kissinger overnight for his reference

84. Ji Chaozhu-U.S. Embassy Officer, March 2, 1982.

(Kissinger, 1979, pp. 748–749). Premier Zhao Ziyang once noted to President Reagan, as presumed proof of Soviet designs on Taiwan, that Moscow television had recently carried a film clip of Taiwan President Chiang Ching-kuo officiating at a National Day (October 10) celebration in Taipei.[85] And during the arms-sales negotiation in early 1982, Vice Foreign Minister Zhang Wenjin began a session with Assistant Secretary of State John Holdridge by complaining that "last night's ABC news broadcast" had carried a report that President Reagan had decided to sell F-5E aircraft to Taiwan.[86]

The point of these examples is that the Chinese have long had timely access to the full range of foreign news media, whose reports are rapidly translated and circulated within the political elite in the internal *(nei-bu)* publications *Reference News* and *Reference Materials* and other information media of which we may be unaware. The PRC embassies clearly have a press-reporting function, which includes timely assessment of U.S. congressional debates. Zhang Wenjin, for example, protested to the U.S. embassy in Beijing about congressional consideration of sales of the F-X fighter aircraft to Taiwan based on statements made by Senator John Glenn and Congressman Clement Zabloki on August 21 and 31, 1981.[87]

Several observations should be made about the impact of this rapid access to foreign news media on PRC negotiating behavior as revealed in the official record of U.S.-PRC exchanges. First, foreign press materials are not only intended to keep the leadership and lower-level party cadre informed of world events, they also are used to inform them—in an oblique and deniable fashion—of policy changes within the PRC government itself. Middle-level government officials have reported that they first anticipated a major change in China's America policy when they read a translation of Mao's *Life* magazine interview, which had been circulated in *Reference Materials*.[88] The Zhou Enlai inter-

85. Reagan-Zhao, October 21, 1981.

86. Zhang Wenjin-Holdridge, January 11, 1982.

87. Zhang-Freeman, September 9, 1981.

88. Personal communication.

view with James Reston in August 1971 was similarly given wide circulation within China—thus feeding back to the cadre changes in policy of which they may not have been aware from domestic sources.

Second, while we do not know the editorial procedures by which foreign media reports are selected for inclusion in limited-circulation internal publications, it is rather clear that the top leadership does *not* edit out reports that could be harmful to its promotion of certain policies. Relevant examples are legion: Deng complained to Secretary of State Haig in June 1981 about reports that President Reagan's daughter was visiting Taiwan, noting that this was a very sensitive issue in China.[89] And he complained to former Vice President Mondale a few months later that public statements by U.S. officials on the F-X (experimental fighter aircraft) issue were complicating his handling of the Taiwan arms-sales question within the PRC.[90] Vice Foreign Minister Zhang Wenjin, in an exchange with Assistant Secretary of State Holdridge on the arms-sales issue, expressed frustration and resentment about the way the American press discussed Taiwan and the PRC:

> *You have . . . expressed hope that China will reduce criticism of U.S. arms sales to Taiwan in the press, but this matter concerns China's sovereignty and independence. In the United States, both the press and officials frequently disclose news on this situation. You have told us not to pay attention to this, but afterwards the news turns out to be true. In the U.S. press, there are many articles tantamount to malicious attacks on China. These violate the agreement on the establishment of diplomatic relations. In many newspaper commentaries, Taiwan is looked on as a country, an ally, and China is maliciously attacked. The Chinese people are very sensitive about such criticism and have exercised great restraint. We cannot stop the expression of the Chinese people's feelings in the press. It is simply impossible for the Chinese press not to write about it. There are letters from readers which have expressed much stronger opposition, but we don't want them published. I would like to give some advice. I hope the U.S. press will adopt a more prudent and restrained attitude and stop malicious attacks on China. I don't want to give spe-*

89. Deng-Haig, June 16, 1981.

90. Deng-Mondale, November 22, 1981.

> *cific examples. You know [what they are]. But so long as the U.S. press continues to attack China in this way, there will be a limit to China's restraint.*[91]

No doubt there was a certain amount of playacting in Zhang's protest, for he understood full well that the U.S. government cannot control private press writings about China; yet private statements made by Foreign Ministry officials at the conclusion of the arms-sales negotiation indicate that U.S. press materials distributed in China through *Cankao Xiaoxi*—especially when a party plenum or congress or a National People's Congress meeting is in session—can stir up political pressures that the leadership finds difficult to control.

The extent to which the PRC political process has become sensitized to U.S. press reporting is perhaps best summed up by a 1983 incident in which a mild Foreign Ministry protest to the U.S. government about an arms-sales decision for Taiwan was characterized in the U.S. press as pro forma. This story was circulated in China, and a few days later the PRC registered a second, much sharper protest—apparently because of pressures generated within the PRC by the first account.[92]

The Power of Words

A distinguishing characteristic of the Chinese political process noted by a number of foreign analysts is the unusual power attributed to the use of words in asserting political authority.[93] Mastery of calligraphy and the esoteric classical language and memorization of the writings of Confucius were the primary skills of the traditional political elite, the scholar-officials of imperial times. Even during the Communist era, Mao Zedong asserted his authority through required study of his writings (as in the Party rectification movements begun in Yanan during the 1930s) and through mass incantations from the "little red book" of his quotations during the Cultural Revolution.

---

91. January 11, 1982.

92. See *Washington Post,* June 6, July 20, and July 24, 1983.

93. See Lifton (1968), pp. 63–65, and Pye (1968), pp. 109, 411–412.

China's ideographic written language, with its mystical origins in bone divination, also seems to sensitize the Chinese to symbolic forms of communication. Chinese leaders are aware of the way their ancient language, for all its cultural richness and its role in unifying the country, has hindered China's modernization. As Zhou Enlai commented to Henry Kissinger in their first encounter: "With respect to China's long history, there's one good point, the written language, which contains a heritage of 4,000 years based on historical relics. This is beneficial to the unification and development of our nation. But there's also a weak point. Our symbolic language of ideograms restricted our development. You might think that these are all idle words, but they are not. They show that we know our objective world and we can coolly appraise it."[94]

In politics, the Chinese are masters of the symbolic act and of the communicating power of a well-turned phrase. At the beginning of the normalization phase of the U.S.-PRC relationship, most American observers missed the significance of Mao's reception of his American "old friend" Edgar Snow atop *Tian An Men* on National Day, 1970[95]—yet this was the first overt sign of the chairman's intention to initiate a dialogue with U.S. officials. More familiar to American observers in the evolution of the relationship are the symbols of ping-pong diplomacy in the spring of 1971, China's use of its panda bears to create an atmosphere of friendship, and the development of such verbal symbols as "the Shanghai Communiqué," "firing empty cannons," "hegemony" and "the Polar Bear," the "Japanese model" of normalization, the "nine points" for peaceful reunification with

94. Zhou-Kissinger, July 9, 1971.

95. One problem in U.S.-PRC relations has been the tendency of the two sides to misinterpret communications, especially those of a symbolic nature. Each side probably tends to overinterpret "signals" of the other, or to assume a purposeful calculation behind some word or act when none was intended. For example, Mao himself once indicated to Kissinger his overreading of the intention behind President Nixon's reception of a PRC acrobatic troupe at the White House. Said Mao: "From the atmosphere with which your President received our acrobatic troupe, I thought that the Vietnamese issue was going to be settled" (Mao-Kissinger, February 17–18, 1973).

Taiwan, and "the dark cloud" [of Taiwan arms sales] hanging over the relationship.

This distinctive use of language in the political process is expressed in a number of ways in Chinese negotiating behavior. The Chinese are meticulous record keepers, and the words spoken across the green baize table in negotiating exchanges acquire the weight of a formal commitment. Zhou's repeated assertion to Kissinger that "our word counts" expresses a sense that integrity is judged by one's willingness to honor one's word.[96] Chinese negotiators are quick to cite the past record of exchanges to assert that their commitment to a principled position is unchanged—as in Deng Xiaoping's 1974 invocation of Chairman Mao's words to justify his rejection of Kissinger's approach to completing normalization at that time, or in Huang Hua's rebuff of Secretary of State Haig's complaint in 1981 that the PRC was escalating its demands for an end to U.S. arms sales to Taiwan in which Huang cited Deng's statement that the arms-sales issue would have to be discussed in the future.[97]

Chinese negotiators readily cite their counterparts' own words to hold them to a position they might want to change. And they invoke the words of a counterpart's predecessors to reject a change in policy. After reading from the Deng-Ford exchanges of 1975, Deng asserted that Vance's presentation on normalization was a "retreat" from the position stated by his predecessors.[98]

The Chinese are skillful in using vague formulations to draw out a negotiating counterpart so that his position is on the record; and when they are in an intransigent mood, they will reiterate their policy with great tenacity and, to assert the authority of their own position, will insist on having the last word in an exchange.[99]

96. The Chinese, for the most part, are meticulous in translating statements negotiated in English into Chinese. This was Kissinger's experience in constructing the Shanghai Communiqué (see Kissinger, 1979, pp. 1084–1085).

97. Haig-Huang Hua, October 23, 1981.

98. Deng-Vance, August 24, 1977.

99. Two almost humorous examples of PRC negotiators dragging out exchanges to ensure that they have the last word are contained in Johnson (1984), pp. 246–247, and Beam (1978), p. 125.

Word Games (Style of Argumentation)

Chinese officials, like all negotiators, observe certain stylized conventions in official exchanges. Some verbal conventions are virtually universal in communicating intentions or in imparting second- and third-order meanings to words spoken. Table 2 summarizes some of the verbal conventions found in the normalization record that are familiar to any diplomat with substantial international experience. But there are certain forms of argumentation characteristic of Chinese negotiating practice that are, if not unique, at least highly distinctive.

"You're Violating the Principles of the Relationship!"

Having worked assiduously in the early phase of a negotiation to gain a counterpart government's commitment to certain general principles, the PRC negotiator will use that commitment to constrain his interlocutor's actions as the relationship evolves. In the U.S.-PRC relationship, this pressure tactic was most evident with regard to the issue of U.S. arms sales to Taiwan. In 1978, as the normalization negotiations entered their final phase, PRC officials protested each Carter administration sale to the island as a violation of the principles embodied in the Shanghai Communiqué.

This same plaint of violation of principle was Beijing's primary form of verbal pressure during the arms-sales communiqué negotiation in 1982. And while the joint communiqué of August 1982 on arms sales and the tacit understandings on the issue that were part of the normalization dialogue constitute a framework and a set of expectations for handling the issue, the Chinese are likely to exert future pressures on the United States by asserting that the United States is violating the principles of the relationship. As Premier Zhao Ziyang declared in a major policy statement of 1983 (Zhao Ziyang, 1983, p. xxiv):

> *The United States has formulated the so-called "Taiwan Relations Act" and continues to sell arms to Taiwan in serious violation of the public commitments it undertook in all the Sino-U.S. communiqués and the principles governing the establishment of Sino-U.S. diplomatic relations that both parties agreed to. (Zhao Ziyang, 1983, p. xxiv)*

Table 2. Pressuring Phrases in Chinese Negotiating Parlance

Phrase	Meaning
"Speaking personally . . ." **"It is my personal view that . . ."**	Signifies an unofficial but on-the-record comment, usually of a critical nature, that the negotiator wants considered by his counterpart, but one that he should not be held accountable for as a formal governmental position or have quoted back to him in future negotiating sessions.
"To be frank . . ." **"Speaking very candidly . . ."**	Signifies a serious, usually critical statement, often with an implicit threat of some unfavorable development if the critical comment is not taken seriously.
"I have been instructed to tell you that . . ." **"I have been authorized [directed] by the Premier to inform you that . . ."**	Communicates a policy position, usually of a demanding or threatening nature, that carries the weight of a formal or collective decision by the leadership.
"It is our principled position that . . ."	Signifies an inflexible negotiating position from which the PRC will not budge (at a particular stage of a negotiation). When no mention is made of principle, the negotiator is usually prepared to be flexible in working out "concrete arrangements."
"Having taken your views into account, it is our position that . . ."	Signifies that the PRC has made some adjustment of its position to reflect the views of its negotiating counterpart but does not intend to compromise further.
"It is up to the doer to undo the knot."	The counterpart government is responsible for a certain situation, and China will do nothing to resolve the problem.
"If you do X, your side will bear all the consequences." **"If you do Y, it will have a very bad effect on our relationship."**	A direct, but unspecified threat to take retaliatory action in response to a specific action on the part of the counterpart government.
"If you do X, China will not stand idly by."	The ultimate threat of action, usually of a military nature, in response to the specified behavior on the part of the counterpart government.

"We Don't Need You; You Need Us!"

PRC negotiating rhetoric also reflects the relationship game that, for the Chinese, is the psychological core of the political process. As the U.S.-PRC relationship has deepened, the Chinese have sought to ease their anxieties about once again becoming dependent on a more powerful, yet distrusted, foreign power by asserting with great conviction—if not convincing logic—that they are part of the Third World, or that they pursue an independent foreign policy. And at times when PRC leaders have felt the United States was not carrying its weight in the relationship, or when they feared becoming too dependent on the United States, they have asserted with even greater vehemence that it is the United States that needs a relationship with China and not vice versa (and thus the United States should fulfill its part of the relationship).

"You're Guilty, at Fault; You Owe China a Debt!"

A pressure tactic that is hardly unique to the Chinese, yet nonetheless is characteristic of their negotiating rhetoric, is their tendency to lay blame or find fault as a basis for pressing their interlocutors for some action that will accommodate their interests. In the normalization dialogue, this tactic was particularly evident in discussions on the Taiwan issue. As Zhou said to Kissinger at the outset of their first encounter, "The question of Taiwan becomes one regarding which we cannot but blame your government."[100] Deng picked up this theme in the mid-1970s, not so much because of alleged past U.S. sins on the Taiwan issue, but to pressure Kissinger to follow through on President Nixon's unrealized intention to complete the normalization process in his second term. In October 1975, Foreign Minister Qiao Guanhua sought to put Kissinger on the defensive by commenting that China was prepared to complete the normalization process but the United States was delaying progress because of its political difficulties with the issue. Said Qiao, "It would be good if we can achieve [some progress

100. Zhou-Kissinger, July 9, 1971.

toward normalization]. We understand you have problems. We have no problems."[101]

The Chinese have similarly attempted to play guilt games with the United States on the issue of technology transfers, in order to move the U.S. government to adopt a more forthcoming policy toward the PRC. In late 1981, Deng complained to Secretary of the Treasury Donald Regan that "America has not given China a single item of advanced technology." Citing the failure to follow through on its decision of 1979 to provide the PRC with a census computer, Deng observed,

> *Perhaps the problem is one of how the U.S. treats China. I wonder whether the United States is still not treating China as a hostile country?! . . . We have been waiting. Frankly, we have been very patient. I first raised this matter [of the census computer] eight years ago with Kissinger.*[102]

It is evident that the Chinese maintain a record of grievances which they recite to an interlocutor whom they want to put on the defensive, and they are quick to blame others for problems they cannot resolve.

"You Are Weak; You Are Fearful!"

In the past, some of the most biting Chinese attacks on U.S. policy were assertions that the United States was fearful of the Soviet Union and was displaying weakness by appeasing Moscow through policies of détente—a form of provocation. It is as if the Chinese believed that the best way to move the United States to adopt a more forceful policy against the Soviets was to provoke officials with a challenge to their political toughness.

In late 1971, after President Nixon had decided to assist China if it came under Soviet pressures in the context of a confrontation between India and Pakistan (Kissinger, 1979, pp. 905–910), Huang Hua criticized U.S. policy toward Indian military actions against Pakistan as "weak" and asserted that "one must not

101. Kissinger-Qiao, September 28, 1975.

102. Deng-Regan, November 19, 1981.

show the slightest sign of weakness" in dealing with the Indians and their Soviet backers.[103]

Throughout the Nixon and Ford administrations, the Chinese adopted an ever more critical posture toward U.S. dealings with the Soviet Union, focusing their attacks on the various treaties and agreements that embodied the policy of détente. These verbal attacks—presumably designed to encourage the United States to adopt a posture of unalloyed confrontation toward the Russians—came to a head in 1975–1976 as the Chinese attacked the attitude of "appeasement" which, they said, was increasingly prevalent in "the West." This attack reached its most extreme point in the following exchange between Kissinger and Foreign Minister Qiao Guanhua in the fall of 1976:

> Kissinger: *You said in your speech [to the U.N. General Assembly] that when the U.S. negotiates with the Soviets it is engaging in appeasement and pushing the Soviets toward China. But when the U.S. resists the Soviets, it is engaging in a rivalry of the superpowers against which all mankind should unite. Under those conditions we are playing under rules where we cannot possibly win. . . .*
>
> Qiao: *Your comments are too general. We are never against negotiations with the Soviet Union. We are negotiating with them now. We are not opposed to negotiations. The problem is the basic position from which one negotiates. You will recall that Chairman Mao discussed with you the problem of the Helsinki Conference. After Helsinki the Soviets went on a large scale offensive in Angola, and we believe this was caused by the weak attitude you adopted at Helsinki toward the Soviets. . . . Our view is that the Soviets, through Helsinki, see your weakness.*
>
> Kissinger: *Really, Mr. Foreign Minister, I don't want to be impolite, but I don't agree. We are not weak, rather, we are temporarily weak until after our elections. . . . But that will end on November 2.*
>
> Qiao: *I don't want to be impolite. The Soviets, through Helsinki, have come to feel that the West is anxious to reach agreement. . . . We have mentioned our concerns because in our view we cannot adopt a weak attitude toward the Soviet Union.*[104]

103. Kissinger-Huang Hua, December 10, 1971.

104. Kissinger-Qiao, October 8, 1976.

This line of verbal attack continued during the Carter administration, as in Huang Hua's assertion to National Security Adviser Brzezinski that the United States was fearful of the Soviet Union:

> Huang Hua: *Between the Soviet Union and the United States, who is more afraid of whom? The United States is more afraid of the Soviet Union. In Africa, the Soviet Union is making infiltration and expansion and making an open challenge to the United States. This, I think, has something to do with the weak response on the part of the United States. And I think the policy of appeasement can only inflate the ambitions of the Soviet Union for hegemony.*

Such attacks were usually coupled with verbal bravado that China, in contrast, was in no way fearful of the Soviets:

> Huang Hua: *Your excellency has mentioned that one of the strategic goals of the Soviet Union is to encircle China. As a matter of fact, China has never feared encirclement. The Communist Party of China developed and grew strong while encircled. It is impossible to encircle such a big country as China. . . . There is an advantage in having been encircled. That is, it has compelled us to rely on our own efforts to develop our economy.*[105]

"Your Policy Is Illogical" ("Lifting a Rock Only to Drop It on One's Own Foot")

PRC negotiators, with their dialectical sense of logic, are quick to point out instances where U.S. policy or actions—in the Chinese view—actually work to increase the influence and strength of America's adversaries, or where U.S. policies are internally inconsistent. Such criticisms, of course, are intended to induce changes in U.S. policy that will be favorable to Chinese objectives.

Zhou Enlai attacked the U.S. bombing campaign against North Vietnam in 1971 with the argument that the bombing was helping the Soviets to increase their influence in Hanoi.[106] Deng Xiaoping criticized U.S. grain sales and technology exports to the Soviets as inconsistent with the stated U.S. objective of resisting Soviet hegemony.[107] Defense Minister Geng Biao criticized

---

105. Huang Hua-Brzezinski, May 21, 1978.

106. Zhou-Haig, January 3, 1972.

107. See Deng-Kissinger, October 20, 1975.

U.S. pressures on OPEC as helping the Soviets to increase their influence in the Middle East.[108]

"We Don't Care About . . ." (Devaluation)

When PRC negotiators wish to convey the impression that they are impervious to pressures or unwilling to compromise on some issue, they will assert—often not very convincingly—that they do not particularly care about a given situation or about attaining a certain objective.

In a discussion of the Nixon administration policy on China's representation in the United Nations—which would obviously affect the timing if not the manner in which the PRC gained entry to the organization—Zhou Enlai asserted lack of urgent interest in the matter:

> *You must know we do not consider the matter of regaining our seat in the U.N. an urgent matter. We have gone through this for 21 years and we have lived through it. Even if war should break out, we should be able to live through it. Therefore, we do not attach any importance to the U.N. question, and I didn't [even] mention it yesterday.*[109]

In 1975, as the Chinese sought to bring maximum pressure on the Ford administration to complete the normalization process (by withholding the prospect of a successful presidential visit), they asserted that they feared neither Soviet pressures, which might increase with an evident deterioration in the relationship, nor a delay in normalization:

> *The Chinese side would like to state the following in all frankness: As is known to all, it is the self-interest of the United States which guides its international actions. The Chinese side has long made clear that it entertains no illusions about the policy of the U.S. The basis of China's policy has always been independence and self-reliance. China neither fears intimidation nor seeks protection. As for the normalization of relations between China and the U.S., this is the common aspiration of the people of China and the U.S. And it is the U.S. that owes a debt to China.*

108. Geng-Brown, January 7, 1980.

109. Zhou-Kissinger, July 10, 1971.

> *In the past 26 years, in the absence of diplomatic relations with the U.S., the Chinese people have led a life much better than in any other period in China's history. It can be said with certainty that further delay in the establishment of diplomatic relations between China and the U.S. will not cause the sky to fall, and the 800 million Chinese people will continue to enjoy their happy life. . . . Frankly, the Chinese side does not care about speculations in other quarters about [the state of] Sino-U.S. relations.*[110]

And in 1978, as the Chinese sensed that the Carter administration was moving to a final negotiating round on normalization and as the PRC faced the prospect of growing tensions with the Soviet Union and Vietnam over Indochina, Deng Xiaoping had to deal with the problem of how to accelerate the normalization negotiations without appearing anxious—which, in the Chinese view, would undercut their bargaining position.

Sharpening Differences (Differentiation)

> Mao Zedong: *We also say . . . that each side has its own means and [has] acted out of its own necessity. That [has resulted] in the two countries acting hand-in-hand [to deal with the Soviet challenge].*
>
> Kissinger: *Yes, we both face the same danger. We may have to use different methods sometimes, but for the same objectives.*
>
> Mao: *That would be good. So long as the objectives are the same, we would not harm you nor would you harm us. And we can work together to commonly deal with a bastard [the Soviets] (laughter). Actually, it would be that sometimes we want to criticize you for a while and you want to criticize us for a while. That, your President said, is the ideological influence. You say, "Away with you communists." We say, "Away with you imperialists." Sometimes we say things like that. It would not do* not *to do that.*
>
> Kissinger: *I think both of us must be true to our principles. And in fact it would confuse the situation if we spoke the same language. I have told the Prime Minister that in Europe you, because of your principles, can speak more firmly than we can, strangely enough.*[111]

One of the more intriguing aspects of the U.S.-PRC political association that developed during the 1970s and 1980s was the dialectical quality of cooperation and criticism; the sense of

110. Qiao-Bush, November 4, 1975.

111. Mao-Kissinger, February 17–18, 1973.

shared interests and at the same time an equally sharp sense of the cultural, institutional, and political differences that make the two countries unique. The relationship, in many ways, truly became a matter of "the unity of opposites."

This paradoxical quality became most evident in the negotiating process in the three periods after 1971 when the Chinese purposefully decided to sharpen differences between the two governments: at the time of the drafting of the Shanghai Communiqué in the fall of 1971; in 1974–1976, during the ascendancy of the Gang of Four and the crisis of succession to Mao's leadership; and in 1981–1982 during the negotiations over U.S. arms sales to Taiwan. The political dynamics of these instances of heightened tension are not the same in each instance and are fully known. They reflect in some measure the play of PRC internal politics, especially during the mid-1970s; yet they also are episodes in which the Chinese sought to exert pressure on the United States by drawing a sharp distinction between the positions of the two sides on a range of issues—while not pushing differences to the point of rupturing a fragile association based more on a sense of shared external threat than on common institutions, political values, or developmental objectives.

In October 1971, on Kissinger's second visit to Beijing, during which he initiated exchanges on the joint statement that came to be known as the Shanghai Communiqué, he brought a draft document that "followed the conventional style, highlighting fuzzy areas of agreement and obscuring differences with platitudinous generalizations" (Kissinger, 1979, p. 781). The next day Zhou responded to the draft:

> *Quite uncharacteristically, he made a scorching one-hour speech—at the express direction of Mao, he said. He declared that our approach was unacceptable. The communiqué had to set forth fundamental differences; otherwise, the wording would have an "untruthful appearance." (Kissinger, 1979, p. 781)*

While initially nonplussed at Zhou's sharp attack and his unfamiliar approach to drafting a joint communiqué, Kissinger recalled, "As I reflected further I began to see that the very novelty of the approach might resolve our perplexities. A statement of differences would reassure allies and friends that their interests had been defended; if we could develop some common positions, these would then stand out as the authentic convictions of principled leaders" (Kissinger, 1979, p. 781).

Another instance of sharpening differences occurred in the fall of 1975, during preparations for the Ford presidential visit to the PRC. As noted earlier, the Chinese side sustained their invitation to the American president even as they refused to formulate a visit communiqué that would highlight common positions of the two sides. Foreign Minister Qiao Guanhua told Liaison Office Chief George Bush in the midst of the preparations:

> *We welcome the U.S. side's proposal for a visit to China by President Ford and [we] are prepared to receive him with courtesy. It will be all right whether or not our minds meet. The U.S. side should be clearly aware of this and not harbor any illusions.*[112]

Qiao then related this perspective to the drafting of a joint U.S.-PRC communiqué to mark the conclusion of the presidential visit:

> *The present [U.S.] draft still attempts to cover up differences in principle between China and the U.S. on major international issues and creates a false impression. This will serve neither of our interests. . . . It is unjustifiable to tone down or eliminate language alleged by the U.S. side to be offensive.*

As a negotiating tactic, this approach produced a complex set of effects for both sides: It enabled both parties to assert visibly and sharply their principled positions—which, as Kissinger noted, enabled them to reassure both allies *and domestic constituencies* that their interests were supported in the negotiations; it also put the relationship under considerable strain and forced both sides to define very precisely the value to each of the association. There was a clear limit in each of the above-mentioned instances beyond which Chinese pressures would have strained the relationship to a breaking point; but in each instance, partial compromises on both sides preserved a core of agreement amid the differences. As Mao—a master of this tactic—liked to assert, big quarrels can produce even greater unity.[113]

112. Qiao-Bush, October 31, 1975.

113. Deng-Ford, December 2, 1975.

Debunking (Rejection)

PRC negotiators can be quite sharp in debunking the policies of their counterparts to bring pressure on them to change their positions. A few examples from the record will convey the flavor of their often-ridiculing approach to rejecting the opposite side's views.

In 1974, Deng Xiaoping—speaking to a U.S. congressional delegation—debunked Henry Kissinger's assertions that Soviet pressures against China would reach a high point in the mid-1970s:

> *Often we read in the American press or have heard from American visitors that the Soviets will launch an all-out attack at such and such a time. Last autumn we heard that the attack would come before the rivers froze. Our view was that this was very unlikely. The winter passed. Next we heard that the Soviets would attack us when the ice melted in March. Well, the thaw came, but not the attack. And now once again from very good sources we hear that the Soviets will attack us before the freeze in October. This once again seems to us very unlikely. But, as it is in the future, we can only wait and see.*[114]

In the fall of 1975, Mao ridiculed Kissinger's assertion that the United States "attaches very great significance" to its relationship with the PRC with the counter that Kissinger's words were "not reliable."[115] The chairman, anxious to see normalization accomplished before he died, sought to pressure Kissinger by saying in effect that he wanted action on normalization, not just words.

In 1977, as Deng Xiaoping sought to move the Carter administration to adopt a policy of more vigorous opposition to the Soviet Union, the Chinese criticized Secretary of State Vance's approach to dealing with the Soviets with near ridicule:

> Vance (to Huang Hua): *I understand you are going to Kinshasa on the way home, Mr. Minister.*
>
> Huang: . . . *You should go also . . . but I doubt you will—you may be apprehensive of offending the Soviet Union.*[116]

---

114. Deng-Fulbright Codel, September 5, 1974. Deng's purpose was to deflate what he saw as pressure tactics from the United States based on an exaggerated assessment of the Soviet threat to PRC security.

115. Mao-Kissinger, October 21, 1975.

116. Vance-Huang Hua, June 2, 1978.

In an effort to put off movement on the normalization issue in the summer of 1977—and to position China more favorably for eventual discussion of the subject—Deng debunked Secretary Vance's presentation on the subject as "a retreat, not a step forward" from the position put forward by the Ford administration.[117]

Personal Abuse (Challenging Motives, Sincerity)

In the normalization negotiations, American officials—with a few exceptions—were spared the personal abuse and invective that characterized U.S.-PRC negotiations during the adversarial days of the 1950s and 1960s.[118] In the later efforts of the PRC to build a relationship with the United States, the Chinese capacity for cultured graciousness was the rule, not the exception. At times when they wanted to build pressure on the United States, however, their negotiators showed flashes of the capacity for personal abuse that so dominated the atmosphere of the talks at Panmunjom and Warsaw. Indeed, the contrast between the usual *politesse* of the Chinese and their occasional resort to abusive language and the challenging of motives makes those tactics even more effective.

The first example of sharply challenging motives in the normalization record was Zhou Enlai's assertion to Henry Kissinger in February 1973 that the United States "wants to reach out to the Soviet Union by standing on Chinese shoulders," an accusation to which Mao (the author of the image) added, "I suspect the whole of the West has such an idea, that is to push Russia eastward, mainly against us and also Japan."[119]

During the time of the Gang of Four, PRC diplomats adopted an increasingly acerbic tone in exchanges with U.S. counterparts,

---

117. Deng-Vance, August 24, 1977.

118. Ambassador Kenneth Young has summarized the style of PRC negotiators in that era in the following way: "Glorifying martial virtues and military tactics, the Sinocentric, Maoist and revolutionary diplomat considers negotiation, at least with Americans, an eventual death struggle for the adversary and not a joint benefit for both parties. He has no feeling for his American adversary nor any interest in his case. He indulges in the language of invective and exhausts the vocabulary of the extreme" (Young, 1968, p. 363).

119. Mao-Kissinger, February 17–18, 1973.

no doubt a reflection of political tensions arising from the domestic Chinese political polarization of the time. In the spring of 1974, PRC officials rejected a U.S. warning about the possible attachment of a PRC aircraft scheduled to fly from Beijing to New York for a special session of the United Nations General Assembly, because of the unresolved private-claims/blocked-assets issue.[120] A formal note charged that the United States was engaging in blackmail on the issue. In the summer of 1976, Liaison Office Chief Huang Zhen directly attacked Senator Hugh Scott in a discussion with Secretary of State Kissinger, asserting that the senator had created a "premeditated pretext" to issue a "flagrant threat" to Vice Premier Zhang Chunqiao when he had told the vice premier the previous month that a PRC resort to force to solve the Taiwan issue would harm the development of U.S.-PRC relations.[121]

Distorting the Record

While the Chinese do not hesitate to hold their negotiating counterparts accountable for the words they have spoken into the official record, and despite Zhou's self-righteous assertions that "our word counts," PRC officials have frequently distorted the record of official exchanges with the United States to influence important aspects of the relationship in a direction favorable to their interests. Thus, U.S. negotiators must be as meticulous as the Chinese in maintaining and drawing upon the formal record of past exchanges in negotiating encounters.

One of the U.S. formulations in drafting the Shanghai Communiqué that most impressed the Chinese was the indirect manner in which the issue of the unity of China and Taiwan's relationship to the PRC was expressed: "The United States *acknowledges (renshidao)* that all Chinese on either side of the Taiwan Strait maintain there is but one China and that Taiwan is a part of China. The United States does not challenge that position." It is clear from subsequent comments made by Chinese officials

120. See PRC Liaison Office communications with the Department of State, March 25, March 29, and March 30, 1974.

121. Kissinger-Huang Zhen, August 18, 1976.

that this wording was seen in Beijing as being quite clever, for it avoided a *direct* U.S. affirmation of the unity of China; indeed, one may speculate that the phrasing elicited criticism within the Chinese political system, since Chinese officials later attempted to assert that the United States had *directly* acknowledged or *recognized (chengrenle)* that Taiwan was a part of China or the PRC.

When Secretary of State Kissinger introduced PRC Liaison Office Chief Huang Zhen to his successor Cyrus Vance in early 1977, the following exchange occurred:

> Kissinger: *We negotiated the Shanghai Communiqué, Cy, usually in the evenings after banquets; and after a few* maotais *I did most of the negotiating in Chinese (laughter).*
>
> Huang Zhen: *Some of the wordings in the Shanghai Communiqué were created by you [Kissinger].*
>
> Kissinger: *What impressed the Chinese most about what I have done was the formula we discussed about how to express the idea of one China. We came up with the formula that the Chinese on both sides of the Taiwan Strait maintain that there is only one China, and the U.S. is not disposed to challenge that position.*
>
> Huang Zhen: *In the Shanghai Communiqué, as you mentioned, the U.S. recognized that there was only one China and that Taiwan is only a part of China.*[122]

This misstatement of the record, unchallenged even by its author, was notably pronounced during the final months of the normalization negotiations of 1978, when the Chinese attempted to rectify what they found to be the objectionable indirect formulation of the Shanghai Communiqué. In a review of the evolution of U.S.-PRC relations with U.S. Liaison Office Chief Leonard Woodcock on August 11, 1978, Foreign Minister Huang Hua asserted that in the Shanghai Communiqué the United States "recognized one China and that Taiwan is an integral part of Chinese territory, that is, an integral part of the People's Republic of China."[123] And on December 5, Acting Foreign Minister Han Nianlong told Woodcock that the PRC was prepared to

122. Kissinger-Huang Zhen, January 8, 1977.

123. Huang Hua-Woodcock, August 11, 1978.

normalize U.S.-PRC relations at an early date inasmuch as the United States, he asserted, "had pledged to support the principle of one China and that Taiwan Province is a part of the People's Republic of China."[124]

In the final version of the joint U.S.-PRC communiqué on the establishment of diplomatic relations, the United States slightly modified its indirect formulation of the Shanghai Communiqué to read: "The United States of America acknowledges the Chinese position that there is but one China and Taiwan is part of China." But the Chinese, in translating the English language working text of the communiqué, used the word *chengren* to translate "acknowledge" rather than the phrase *renshidao* which had been used to translate the same word in the Shanghai Communiqué.

The issue of timing for Taiwan's reunification has not been raised directly with the United States in recent years, although Deng, in a speech to party cadre in January 1980, identified "reunification" as one of the three major tasks for the PRC in the 1980s (Deng Xiaoping, 1980).

Another, and in some ways still puzzling, distortion of the official record was the Chinese public assertion in the fall of 1980 that the United States had promised to end all arms sales to Taiwan within a period of a few years. This issue first surfaced after the 1980 presidential election, when Vice Foreign Minister Zhang Wenjin, in a highly unusual action for a PRC official, told the *Washington Post* in an on-the-record interview that "any [American] arms deliveries at all [to Taiwan] violates the normalization agreement."[125] Zhang added, according to the *Post* reporter, that "the United States had told Peking that the problem of arms deliveries to Taiwan would disappear with the passage of time."

These assertions subsequently fueled a number of American press stories on the subject, ultimately provoking former President Jimmy Carter to state publicly, while on a tour of China in August

124. Han Nianlong-Woodcock, December 5, 1978.

125. The *Washington Post,* November 22, 1980.

1981, that he had never told the Chinese that American arms sales to Taiwan would end within a period of a few years.[126]

What was the reason for this provocative distortion of the official record of U.S.-PRC understandings regarding arms sales to Taiwan? The underlying motivation seems to have been a PRC effort to block the realization of their worst fears—that a newly elected Reagan administration would upgrade relations with Taiwan and vigorously implement those provisions of the U.S.-Taiwan Relations Act that called for enabling the island to maintain its defenses. As noted earlier, the Chinese reacted strongly in the pre-election period to statements by candidate Reagan that he intended to reestablish official U.S. relations with Taiwan and make the Taiwan Relations Act the basis of his China policy; and vice presidential candidate Bush's efforts of August 1980 to put Chinese fears to rest, in Deng's words, had not eased their concerns.

Time Pressures (Deadlines)

A final pressure tactic, which is as pronounced in Chinese negotiating behavior as the tendency to play adversaries against one another, is the effort to control the pace of a negotiation so that the counterpart government must make its final decisions under the pressure of a time deadline.

We noted earlier the sensitivity of PRC officials to the rhythms of the political process—to those of their negotiating counterparts as well as their own. The Chinese try to position themselves in a negotiation so that they can control the pace of the exchanges and thus maximize their ability to press their counterpart against a deadline, or at least avoid being time-pressured themselves. At the beginning of the final round of normalization discussions, Liaison Office Chief Leonard Woodcock proposed to his counterpart, Foreign Minister Huang Hua, that they meet

---

126. See *The New York Times*, August 27, 1981. When Zhang and Han were pressed on their allegations by State Department officials and former members of the Carter administration, they admitted that there was nothing in the official record that amounted to U.S. commitment to end arms sales to Taiwan within a brief period of time.

regularly every two weeks to lay out their respective positions. Huang rejected this regular schedule in favor of an arrangement whereby meeting dates would be set as the negotiations proceeded—an arrangement designed, no doubt, to enable Beijing to control the pace of the exchanges.[127]

Chinese officials negotiate with the latent assumption that to be anxious to conclude a deal is to be put at a significant psychological disadvantage. In their political tradition, moreover, those in positions of leadership are supposed to display their authority by a posture of slow-moving reserve (Pye, 1968, pp. 102, 129). And as Henry Kissinger observed of China's most famous Communist mandarin and archetypical negotiator, Zhou Enlai, the premier projected a dignified and relaxed quality of "inner serenity" (Kissinger, 1979, p. 744). Thus, the Chinese will attempt to create the impression that they are in no hurry to conclude an agreement, even when in fact they are under considerable time pressure. For instance, in the first formal and direct communication between Zhou and the Nixon administration, the premier asserted:

> *The Chinese government reaffirms its willingness to receive publicly in Beijing a special envoy of the President of the U.S. (for instance, Mr. Kissinger) or the U.S. Secretary of State or even the President of the U.S. himself for direct meeting and discussions. Of course, if the U.S. President considers that the time is not yet right the matter may be deferred to a later date.*[128]

And at the first formal negotiating session on normalization in 1978, Huang Hua began the discussion with an apology for the delay in scheduling the meeting by noting that he had been preoccupied with the visit of the Minister of Foreign Affairs and Trade of Papua-New Guinea—an aside designed to create the impression that China was in no great hurry to get the negotiations with the United States under way.[129]

---

127. Huang Hua-Woodcock, July 5, 1978 and July 14, 1978.

128. Kissinger-Hilaly, April 27, 1971.

129. Huang-Woodcock, July 5, 1978.

This compulsion to appear unhurried can produce some almost comical formulations when the Chinese are, in fact, anxious to accelerate the pace of a negotiation. The classical expression of such ambivalence is Deng's observation to Kissinger in the fall of 1974:

> *We can sum up our views [on normalization] in two sentences: According to our wishes we would like this matter to come more quickly; but secondly we are not so much in a hurry. . . . If we are able to reach a point acceptable to both sides in a relatively quicker period of time we would welcome this. But Chairman Mao has also said in his talk with the Doctor that we pay special attention to international issues.*[130]

Establishing a deadline for agreement is a process unique to each particular negotiation, but as the following examples show, U.S. officials—with their typically American instinct to resolve issues expeditiously and get on to new challenges—have repeatedly trapped themselves in time deadlines.

In the negotiation of the Shanghai Communiqué, while most of the text had been agreed upon during Kissinger's October 1971 visit to Beijing, resolution of the critical formulation dealing with Taiwan was delayed until the Nixon presidential visit. The Chinese rejected a formulation on the issue brought by Kissinger's deputy, Alexander Haig, during the January 1972 advance trip, and they held out on this highly sensitive issue until the presidential party's last day in Beijing. Kissinger later recalled of his 20 hours of negotiation with Vice Foreign Minister Qiao Guanhua during the Nixon visit, "Each side pushed the other against the time limit [of the President's scheduled departure from the Chinese capital] to test whose resiliency was greater. Determination was masked by extreme affability. The best means of pressure available to each side was to pretend that there was no deadline" (Kissinger, 1979, p. 1075). And at one point he and Qiao even discussed the possibility of no communiqué—just to feign willingness to have the visit conclude without a formal agreement.[131] Qiao compromised on the Taiwan formulation

130. Deng-Kissinger, November 26, 1974.

131. Qiao-Kissinger, February 24–25, 1972.

with less than 12 hours remaining before the scheduled departure time.

In the normalization negotiations of 1978, the United States established a time deadline when President Carter and Secretary of State Vance indicated to PRC officials that they were prepared to establish diplomatic relations by the end of the year.[132] The Chinese then paced the Huang-Woodcock exchanges in Beijing over a six-month period so that by early December there had been a full airing of views; yet uncertainty remained about whether or when a final deal might be struck. Vice Foreign Minister Han Nianlong told Woodcock in their meeting on December 5 that Deng was prepared to meet with him "at an early date," yet a week later no meeting had been scheduled, leading National Security Adviser Brzezinski in Washington to call in Liaison Office Chief Chai Zemin on December 12 to indicate that time was running out if they were to meet the January 1, 1979, deadline.[133] The Chinese then scheduled the Deng-Woodcock session within 24 hours.

A similar situation, although with a different outcome, marked the playing out of the arms-sales negotiation of 1981–1982. The United States established a time deadline for agreement by proposing on January 11, 1982, that the two sides negotiate on the issue with the objective of issuing a joint communiqué on the tenth anniversary of the Shanghai Communiqué, February 28. The Chinese thus thought they had a time deadline against which to press the United States; and they stalled the negotiations throughout the first half of February in order to build pressure on the Reagan administration.[134] The administration then decided to let the deadline pass rather than reach an undesirable agreement, ultimately trapping *the Chinese* in a time deadline.

An interesting example of Chinese management of a negotiation to establish a time deadline where none really existed was

---

132. Carter-Chai Zemin, September 19, 1978, and Vance-Huang Hua, October 3, 1978.

133. Brzezinski-Chai, December 11, 1978.

134. See MFA Officials-U.S. Embassy Officer exchange of February 5, 1982, and Zhang Wenjin-Hummell, February 15, 1982.

the PRC-British negotiation of 1982–1984 on the future of Hong Kong. The nearest thing to a "natural" deadline was the 99-year expiration date of the 1898 Sino-British treaty on Hong Kong in 1997; but this distant date put no pressure on the British and, indeed, put the Chinese in a position where they faced an almost open-ended negotiating situation, something that gave the British the time leverage. In order to reverse this situation and put the British under time pressure, the Chinese asserted publicly on November 9, 1983, that unless there was a negotiated agreement by September 1984 they would proceed to issue a unilateral PRC policy on the future of the colony.[135]

End Game

> Qiao Guanhua: *Let us go straight to the point. Following the discussion between the Premier and Dr. Kissinger, and in the spirit of that discussion, and after making a study after that discussion, and before the Premier meets with the President, we have decided to accept your proposal.*[136]

The lengthy period of assessment can end rather abruptly when the Chinese feel they have fully tested the flexibility in their counterpart's position and have concluded that formal agreement serves their purposes. Much in the style of a Chinese painter, who stares at his blank paper at length and then executes his conception with rapid strokes of the brush, the negotiator will quickly conclude an agreement after a protracted assessment of his counterpart's position. The end-game phase of a negotiation is usually brief, businesslike, and conducted at a high level of authority as the negotiators give concrete expression in some formal document to the principles and objectives that have been discussed at length by lower-level officials in the assessment phase.

The Chinese, like all negotiators, face a threefold choice (Iklé, 1964, pp. 59–75): They must either strike a formal agreement on the terms their counterpart is prepared to accept, abort the negotiation, or continue to bargain. In the U.S.-PRC negotiations

135. *The New York Times,* November 10, 1983, and Chang (1983), p. 18.

136. Qiao-Kissinger, February 25–26, 1972.

of the 1970s, there was at least one instance in which the Chinese aborted a negotiation, that on the private-claims/blocked-assets issue. A combination of bureaucratic resistance to concluding an agreement and internal political pressures associated with the rise in influence of the Gang of Four led Beijing to repudiate a solution to the issue worked out in November 1973 by the ailing Zhou Enlai.[137] The more familiar experience in the normalization years, however, was that of the Chinese reaching partial agreements while reserving position on certain aspects of a situation in order to draw the United States into a more active relationship, from which they might improve their bargaining position on the unresolved issues for future rounds of talks.

The negotiating record indicates that PRC negotiators signal very clearly their intent to conclude an agreement, i.e., to shift from assessment to end game. In the normalization negotiation of 1978, PRC officials switched from their stalling tactics of the previous year—a posture of rhetorically asking, "How can it possibly be the case that we are not impatient on such a matter?"[138]—by signaling that Deng Xiaoping was interested in visiting the United States,[139] through outright expressions of impatience,[140] and by indicating in the negotiating sessions an urgent interest in substantive and concrete descriptions of how the positions of the two sides might be reconciled. As Huang Hua said to Leonard Woodcock in their third meeting in the summer of 1978:

> *In order to solve the problem of normalization one should not evade questions of substance, such as what it is that has detracted from the normalization of relations, and the question of how and when the U.S. government will take concrete measures to fulfill the three conditions put forward by the Chinese government.*[141]

137. PRC message of June 14, 1974.

138. Deng-Brzezinski, May 21, 1978.

139. Foreign Minister Huang said to Secretary of State Vance in the summer of 1978, "With regard to the invitation extended by Dr. Brzezinski for the Vice Premier to make a visit to the United States, the Vice Premier said, 'In that case we must work harder, since I am getting old.'" (Vance-Huang, June 2, 1978)

140. PRC Liaison Office Chief Chai Zemin told Assistant Secretary of State Holbrooke on August 16, 1978, that his view on normalization was "the sooner the better." See also Brzezinski-Chai, September 27, 1978.

141. Huang Hua-Woodcock, August 11, 1978.

Such signals of impatience and a desire to go beyond general principles to discuss concrete implementation indicate that Chinese leaders have concluded that an agreement is desirable and within reach. This does not preclude additional hard bargaining over the detailed language of a formal agreement, as the Chinese test to the limit their counterpart's firmness of purpose, and PRC negotiators may even create an apparent deadlock at the eleventh hour. But as Kissinger observed of the final day of negotiations on the Shanghai Communiqué: "In every negotiation a point is reached where both sides have gone too far to pull back. Accumulated mutual concessions create their own momentum; at some stage retreat puts into question the judgment of the negotiators" (Kissinger, 1979, p. 1078).

The most reliable sign that agreement is at hand is the intervention of a senior leadership figure in the negotiation—a political figure would not put his "face" into a negotiation that was about to collapse. On the night of July 10–11, 1971, just hours before his departure from Beijing, Kissinger had a long and frank discussion with Huang of their differences in drafting a public announcement of Kissinger's secret visit to the Chinese capital and Zhou's invitation to President Nixon to visit the PRC. After a midnight break of several hours, Huang reconvened the discussion—while Zhou secretly waited nearby—and tabled a joint statement that required only a one-word change, after which Zhou entered the room for a final exchange of views (Kissinger, 1979, pp. 752–753).

In drafting the Shanghai Communiqué, the same pattern was repeated on the last day of the negotiations in Beijing. As Kissinger recalled: "Zhou joined the negotiation for half an hour that afternoon, a clear indication of his confidence [that an agreement was attainable] . . . and that he would take responsibility for the requisite compromise" (Kissinger, 1979, p. 1078). In December 1978, the Chinese signaled to Leonard Woodcock the approaching finale of the normalization negotiations when his counterpart in the December 4 session, acting Foreign Minister Han Nianlong, concluded the discussion by saying that Deng Xiaoping wanted to meet with him shortly. In the arms-sales negotiation of 1978, an apparent deadlock at the negotiating table on August 14 was paralleled by a statement by Vice Premier Wan Li to a visiting U.S. cabinet official that an agreement would be reached "in the near future."[142] The next day, the Chinese accepted the position of the U.S. negotiator. In the negotiations of early 1984 on a nuclear cooperation agreement, the imminence of a Chinese compromise was likewise signaled to the American negotiator, Ambassador Richard Kennedy, when his Chinese counterpart indicated that Premier Zhao Ziyang would receive him before his imminent departure from Beijing.

While the substantive details of a formal agreement, of course, vary from negotiation to negotiation, there is a high level of consistency to the pattern of the end-game phase of a negotiation with the Chinese: It occurs after a protracted period of exchanges, it almost invariably comes at the eleventh hour of some deadline that is part of the structure of the negotiating context, and it usually involves the intervention of a senior Chinese political figure who will either cut the knot of an apparent deadlock or bless an agreement the negotiators have constructed (with his behind-the-scenes direction). This phase is brief and businesslike.[143]

Two other characteristics of the end game are worth noting. The Chinese will use the occasion of reaching formal agreement to "tag" for the future their position on the issues where they have "reserved position." In the Shanghai Communiqué this "tagging" was accomplished in their unilateral paragraphs on the issues of Taiwan and various international problems. In the normalization agreement, Deng Xiaoping's final session with Leonard Woodcock concluded with Deng's assertion that the arms-sales issue should be discussed in the future (see the Deng-Woodcock exchange of December 15, 1978). And the unilateral public statement by

---

142. Wan Li-Samuel Pierce, August 14, 1982.

143. Several former American officials interviewed for this project commented that there was an almost anticlimactic quality to the final period of constructing a formal agreement with the Chinese, coming as it tends to do after months of exchanges or an intense period of days or weeks of negotiation. Kissinger's observation about how easy the final drafting of the communiqué for his July 1971 visit was is echoed in Woodcock's characterization of his negotiation with Deng of the text of the normalization agreement of December 13, 1978.

Premier Hua Guofeng reaffirmed PRC opposition to U.S. arms sales to Taiwan and the position that the manner of reunifying Taiwan with "the motherland" was an internal Chinese matter.

It should also be noted that the Chinese have a preference for political agreements cast in the form of relatively vague expressions of principle and intent, and made public in the form of joint press statements, communiqués, or joint declarations, as opposed to formal treaties or highly specific, "contractual" arrangements. This seems to reflect not only a preference for the flexibility that relatively vague language affords them in future negotiating rounds or in subsequent efforts to press the counterpart government to implement the "spirit" of an agreement, but also their distrust of legalistic approaches to politics and the underlying assumption of the relationship game that good *guanxi* and a strong sense of shared interest are the most reliable guarantors of a political agreement.

Implementation

The implementation of a negotiated agreement is not usually thought of as part of the negotiating process; yet the Chinese press their counterparts to an agreement for "strict implementation."

The United States began to experience PRC pressures regarding the implementation dimension of the U.S.-PRC relationship in the summer of 1973, when Zhou Enlai commented to Liaison Office Chief David Bruce that the relationship would develop most effectively if "one keeps one's promises" regarding normalization and opposition to the Soviet Union. More-direct pressure on the normalization issue was raised first in 1974, in Qiao Guanhua's low-key comment to Bruce that the recent appointment of a new U.S. ambassador to Taipei and the opening of two new Republic of China consulates in the United States represented "minor problems" in the relationship.[144] The most intense pressures for implementation of the 1972 Nixon expression of intent to complete normalization in the second term came (as detailed earlier) in the fall of 1975. Yet the Chinese

144. Qiao-Bruce, April 2, 1974.

pressed Kissinger obliquely, with the threat of an unsuccessful Ford presidential visit, rather than by complaining directly about the U.S. failure to meet the Nixon time schedule.

The Chinese were delicate in pressing the Carter administration to follow through on the normalization time commitment of its predecessor,[145] although, as noted earlier, they did hold Secretary Vance and National Security Adviser Brzezinski to the *terms* agreed to by President Ford.[146] Once normalization was accomplished, the Chinese began to press on implementive aspects of the new relationship.

While the Chinese posture themselves as self-righteous sticklers in overseeing the implementation of agreements, they in fact have a less-than-perfect record in following through. They reneged on the agreement worked out between Zhou Enlai and Kissinger in 1973 to resolve the private-claims/blocked-assets issue; and having agreed with Secretary of State Haig in the summer of 1981 to send General Liu Huaqing to the United States for talks on arms-transfer issues, they withdrew the arrangement with complaints about U.S. arms sales to Taiwan. And in the spring of 1984, Premier Zhao Ziyang, in a discussion with President Reagan, laid the basis for eventual nonfulfillment of the U.S.-PRC grain-trade agreement.

U.S. businessmen, in particular, complain frequently about Chinese failures to implement contractual agreements. With their penchant for pressing their friends to "understand" (forgive) their failure to follow through, as well as their inclination to seek substantial modifications of contracts once signed, the Chinese have not maintained a record for meticulously imple-

---

145. President Ford told Deng that after the 1976 election, "we will be in a position to move much more specifically toward the normalization of relations" (Deng-Ford, December 4, 1975).

146. Deng told Brzezinski in the spring of 1978, "President Ford stated [in 1975] that if he was reelected he would move to full normalization according to the three conditions without any reservation. We were very happy at that time with the oral commitment of President Ford. Consequently, President Ford was not reelected, and of course the new administration has a right to reconsider this question" (Deng-Brzezinski, May 21, 1978).

menting agreements that they sign with their political and economic partners.

Personalities

We have thus far described evident patterns in the way PRC officials attempt to manage negotiations as if the process were independent of the personalities involved. While this is true in some measure, inasmuch as culture and institutions tend to dilute the influence of individual actions, personalities can and do significantly shape both the style and the substantive content of negotiating encounters.

In U.S. dealings with the PRC, two factors have tended to magnify the impact of individual personalities: the highly personalized quality of the Chinese political process, and the remarkable continuity of senior personnel in the PRC leadership that has given a few individuals enormous influence over the PRC's foreign relations.

The formal negotiating record assessed for this analysis and the personal memoirs of the American officials who conducted negotiations with PRC counterparts reveal interesting variations in style among the Chinese leaders who managed the relationship with the United States during the 1970s and early 1980s. They also disclose interesting hints about the interrelationships among the various leaders, as well as insights into the state of elite politics in the Chinese capital.

Our objective here is not to present an elaborate assessment of the personalities of the PRC leaders and senior officials who have been the primary managers of the U.S.-PRC relationship, but rather to highlight two points: First, the personalities of individual PRC leaders *do* influence the style in which the negotiating process is managed; and second, given the inevitably personalized quality of face-to-face negotiating (which the Chinese enhance via the games of *guanxi*), American negotiators can be better prepared for their encounters with senior PRC officials if they have informed assessments of the personalities and negotiating styles of their counterparts.

Mao Zedong comes across in the official record, as well as in the Nixon and Kissinger memoirs,[147] as the near-imperial authority he was in China for so many years. His presentational style was highly symbolic, occasionally delphic, and now and then revealing of a peasant crudity that bespoke his social origins.[148] He was the most unconstrained of all the PRC leaders in discussing internal as well as international politics; and he would occasionally take personal digs at his colleagues (terming Qiao Guanhua "Lord Qiao" and characterizing Guo Moro as "a man who worships Confucius"). His presentations set the tone and the political themes for each of the Kissinger and presidential visits during his tenure; his brief but purposeful comments on all topics of concern provided the authority for the presentations of all lower-level officials. And when Zhou Enlai receded from a direct role in the negotiations in late 1973 because of physical illness and political attack, Mao carried the detail of discussions on international events and the Taiwan issue.

While it can only be inferred from the negotiating record, it is evident that Mao directed the tactics as well as the grand strategy of the relationship with the United States. It was at his direction that Zhou discussed with Kissinger the meaning of the Cultural Revolution; and Mao the provocateur directed Zhou to attack Kissinger's initial conciliatory approach to drafting the Shanghai Communiqué in October 1971. The aggressiveness of Mao's personality was evident during the tense year of 1975, when he told Liaison Office Chief George Bush, "You don't know my temperament. I like people to curse me. . . . If you don't curse me, I won't see you. . . ."[149] The chairman's feisty mood clearly suffused the entire Chinese political process in his final year of life.

---

147. See Nixon (1978), pp. 563–580; Kissinger (1979), pp. 2057–2063; and Kissinger (1982), pp. 65–66, 691, 696.

148. For example, Mao asked Kissinger in the fall of 1973 why the American people were always "breaking wind" (*fang pi*) over the Watergate affair—a disparaging characterization that probably reflected Mao's concern with the erosion of Nixon's authority, as it would affect Mao's plans for the normalization of U.S.-PRC relations (Mao-Kissinger, November 12, 1973).

149. Mao-Kissinger, October 21, 1975.

Zhou Enlai is revealed in the official negotiating record not only as the cultured conciliator he was known to be worldwide, but also as an official exceptionally deferential to Mao (Nixon, 1978, pp. 223–236; Nixon, 1980, pp. 217–248; Kissinger, 1979, pp. 742–755). His presentations were laced with references to "Chairman Mao's wise policy" or "Chairman Mao's instructions." His prodigious grasp of history gave him considerable debating ammunition, and he would seek to put his interlocutors on the defensive with facts and critiques of the logic of their policies rather than with bluster or pompous argumentation. Zhou could use self-criticism to great effect. And despite his seniority in the Chinese Communist political order, he showed great discipline and reserve in his presentations on all issues—clearly hewing to Mao's party line.

Zhou operated in tandem with Chairman Mao. One of the unresolved mysteries of the last four years of his (and Mao's) life is whether in the final succession crisis Mao withdrew his decades-long support for Zhou to back the Gang of Four, or whether the infirm chairman himself began to lose his grip over the party radicals.[150]

Qiao Guanhua is projected in the negotiating record as an intellectual clone of Zhou Enlai, but without Zhou's political stature. His presentational style was, like Zhou's, highly intellectualized; and his barely concealed arrogance is clearly the source of the epithet "Lord Qiao." The feisty Deng Xiaoping, even when still vulnerable after recent political rehabilitation, called Qiao to his face a "foreign bumpkin" *(yang baozi)*. When he was expected to apply pressure on an interlocutor, Qiao's presentational style would turn acid and overwhelmingly arrogant—especially in the sessions of October 1975 and his last encounter with Kissinger on October 8, 1976, only a few days before his purge as one who had pandered to the Gang of Four. The six Qiao-Kissinger encounters at the UN in New York City, beginning in the fall of 1972, provide not only a rich elaboration of the key

150. Mao's implicit attack on Jiang Qing in a discussion with Kissinger in early 1973 can be read either as a rejection of the radicals or as an effort to mislead Kissinger (and perhaps Zhou) about where his sentiments and support lay.

strategic issues underlying the U.S.-PRC relationship, but also a clear sequential record of the political mood of the relationship over a five-year period.

Huang Hua is revealed in the negotiating record to be Deng Xiaoping's Zhou Enlai—his "front man." Yet the differences between the urbane and cultured Zhou and the acid-tongued Huang are profound. Huang comes across in the 1978–1982 period as the political "heavy," the bad guy, in contrast to Deng the conciliator. Huang displayed no political or intellectual flexibility in this period, and his presentations were self-righteously nationalistic, pompous, and unyielding. It was Huang who created the apparent deadlock in the arms-sales talks of 1982 that political rationalizer Deng Xiaoping stepped in to resolve.

These brief sketches of the major personalities who confronted U.S. officials across the green baize table in the 1970s and 1980s give only a taste of what can be drawn from the negotiating record in assessing the negotiating styles of individual PRC officials. There is good evidence that the Chinese make detailed assessments of the attitudes and political roles of their negotiating counterparts. The issue for the U.S. government is whether it can better prepare its negotiators for dealings with the Chinese by providing them with more-detailed assessments of the negotiating styles of PRC officials.

4

Counterstrategies and Countertactics[1]

Intellectual understanding of a political counterpart's approach to managing the negotiating process is of limited practical value unless that understanding can be translated into an effective counterstrategy and countertactics. The issue explored in this chapter is whether or not the analysis of PRC negotiating behavior detailed above provides useful insights into ways of dealing more effectively with the Chinese at the negotiating table—and into the broader range of political relationships that contribute to the negotiating process.

While the Chinese have shown considerable skill in controlling the negotiating process and in manipulating their American counterparts in the relationship game, it is possible to conceive

1. Steven R. Pieczenik, a former deputy assistant secretary of state (1976–1979), is due special recognition for his role in conceptualizing this chapter. Dr. Pieczenik is a practicing psychiatrist with extensive negotiating experience in the government and the private sector.

of a general orientation for managing the U.S.-PRC relationship and developing tactical negotiating ploys that will enable American officials to maintain sufficient control of the process to attain U.S. policy objectives. This requires, however, not only an understanding of how the Chinese attempt to manage negotiations and an awareness of effective countering techniques, but also a clear definition of U.S. negotiating objectives and sufficient bureaucratic discipline to implement an appropriate counterstrategy.

The Frustrations of Negotiating with the Chinese

The American negotiators interviewed for this project and the memoirs of U.S. officials who have conducted dealings with PRC counterparts describe a combination of elation and frustration in their dealings with PRC officials. On the one hand, in initial encounters with the Chinese—especially in the early 1970s, when the normalization process began—most U.S. officials were impressed with the cultured dignity, discipline, and purposefulness of senior PRC officials. And virtually all Americans who have dealt with the PRC have found their Chinese counterparts to be personally attractive and highly competent individuals to whom it is easy to relate at a human level. In short, Americans are susceptible to the blandishments of official "friendships" as the Chinese develop them; they are responsive in varying degrees to the games of *guanxi*.

On the other hand, these same officials describe the negative aspects of their negotiating experiences with considerable frustration. To paraphrase their reactions: The Chinese are always lecturing us, presuming that their policies are without doubt correct, while ours are deficient. They assume they have the right to tell us how to run our affairs. They show no hesitation in criticizing the United States and its policies, yet they are self-righteously defensive about any criticism of their own positions. Indeed, for some reason, Americans find it hard to criticize them in the same manner that they criticize us. The Chinese are always getting us to come to them, to negotiate on their home territory and on their terms; they do not send their leaders and negotiating teams to the United States on a reciprocal basis.

The Chinese are remarkably effective in setting a negotiating agenda that serves their purposes and in controlling the timing of the process. They are never satisfied with an agreement, and they never show gratitude for our concessions to their positions; and once an agreement is reached, they invariably press us with additional demands.

These are familiar complaints that reveal the degree to which PRC officials have been able to control the ambience of the negotiating process. And while this is not to say that the United States has been unable to attain its own objectives through negotiations with PRC counterparts, the Chinese have been effective in imparting at least the impression of a no-win quality to certain aspects of the process.

The Chinese try to control the negotiating process by sustaining an air of tension or uncertainty about the relationship. They try to develop a mindset in American officials that the United States "needs" the PRC, while implying that the United States has not been a good "friend of China," that it has not done enough for the relationship, that its policies or actions are either in error or deficient, and that it must do more—on PRC terms—to sustain Chinese good will and cooperation.

The Objective of a Negotiating Counterstrategy and Tactics: Controlling the Process in the Service of U.S. Policy Objectives

The instinctive American reaction to Chinese manipulation of the negotiating relationship is to try to resolve the tension and frustrations of the games of *guanxi*—to either be a good friend or walk away in anger or disgust at the frustrations of the "friendship" manipulations. The American negotiator, as the representative of a technologically oriented, problem-solving culture, wants to eliminate issues, resolve problems, and get on with new challenges. The Chinese negotiator, in contrast, comes from a less-activist cultural background, one which sees management of human relationships as the essence of politics. He assumes that tension and conflicts of interest are enduring aspects of political life requiring skillful and unrelenting management.

This difference in political orientation (explored in more detail in the last section of this chapter) is the basis for the conflict in the approaches of the two cultures to the negotiating process. If the United States is to be more effective in dealings with the Chinese, it must key in on this contrast in orientation. The objective of a negotiating counterstrategy must be not only to reach agreements consonant with American interests, but to gain control of the dynamics, the rhythm, and stratagems of the friendship game as they are expressed in the negotiating process. U.S. management of the relationship must convey to the Chinese an impression of competence in controlling the mechanics of negotiating encounters, an ability to deflect or set limits on their stratagems in the service of reconciling conflicting interests and attaining shared policy objectives.

An effective strategy and competent negotiating tactics may make only a marginal difference in the outcome of a bargaining encounter—nations do not generally conclude agreements that appear not to serve their interests. And a purposeful strategy, if overplayed, can induce distrust or the sense of a game being played simply for the sake of manipulation. Conversely, the *absence* of an adequate counterstrategy is likely to elicit an attitude of disparagement or scorn for a feckless negotiating counterpart. An effectively managed strategy, even one that thwarts Chinese manipulations, can develop a sense of respect for a competent negotiating counterpart. This is the objective that underlies the following exploration of negotiating counterstrategies and tactics.

Strategies of Interdependence, or Autonomy?

In Western practice, nations approach each other as autonomous, equal, and sovereign political entities; but in fact, differences in power—based on resources, geographical position, and national pretensions—lead them to establish hierarchical patterns of policy influence, if not formal alliances, in which one member is in a predominant position. Coalitions of equals, while not unheard of, are more the exception than the rule. Present-day France and West Germany, perhaps, can be viewed as relatively equal partners within the larger NATO coalition,

Table 3. Patterns of Association with the PRC

		National Resources: Subordinate	National Resources: Predominant
Policy Influence	Subordinate	Albania (1960s)	United States (1970s)?
	Predominant	North Korea North Vietnam (1960s->1975)	Soviet Union (1950s)

with the strongly independence-minded French struggling to maintain their autonomy while seeking to benefit from the security and economic benefits of the alliance and the Economic Community.

Beijing's approach to international relations is rooted, as noted at the outset of this study, in the tradition of the imperial tribute system, in which China, as the dominant culture and political power in East Asia, exercised preeminent influence over smaller tributary kingdoms such as Korea and Vietnam. This experience reflects, of course, the dependency/domination pattern fundamental to China's political culture, as we have explored it in terms of the relationship game and its influence on PRC negotiating behavior. Even in China's twentieth-century foreign relations, the pattern of subordination and predominance is evident. This pattern in the PRC's relations with its international partners (the Soviet Union, Albania, and the United States) in the 1950s, 1960s, and 1970s is shown in Table 3.

What does the experience of PRC foreign relations tell us about appropriate American strategies for dealing with China? The key issue is whether we should allow ourselves (however consciously) to be drawn into the relationship game as the Chinese practice it, establish a measure of interdependence with the PRC, or develop a more autonomous pattern that is consonant with American political institutions and practices.

Asymmetries in the American and Chinese Political Cultures

This study is an assessment of *Chinese* negotiating behavior, not U.S. negotiating behavior; yet the record of American dealings with the Chinese says as much about the American political style as it does about the Chinese. Negotiating, after all, is a "binary" process involving the interacting styles and policy concerns of the two sides. Therefore, it is important to highlight some of the stylistic differences between the United States and the PRC that seem to have had a significant impact on the negotiating process. (See Table 4.)

Effective negotiating behavior requires, among other skills, self-awareness of how one's own style and the institutions of one's government are interpreted by the counterpart. It can be argued that some of the major constraints on effective American negotiating performance in dealing with the Chinese are personality quirks of the negotiators and institutional patterns unique to the American system, not Chinese skill in managing the negotiating process. We emphasize that the following interpretation is intended to be suggestive only, to heighten the self-awareness of U.S. negotiating officials. It is not based on any systematic assessment of American negotiating performance and political style.[2]

World Outlook

Americans and Chinese both approach international issues from the perspective of a great power. Developments in virtually all regions of the world are seen as relevant to their security interests, political concerns, and economic development. Elites in both countries assume that history and the weight of their influence destine them for a leadership role in world affairs. For the Chinese, this great-power leadership impulse has been expressed since the founding of the PRC, first in assertiveness within the International Communist Movement during the 1950s, which the Soviets found so galling; then in assertions during the 1960s

2. For a discussion of Chinese and American cultural differences as revealed in commercial negotiating style, see Pye (1982), pp. 13–23 and passim.

Table 4. Asymmetries in the Chinese and American Political Cultures

Category	China	United States	Significance
World outlook	Defensive, indrawing	Expansive, outgoing	Scope of issues
Time perspective	Long-term, historical, passive	Short-term, future-oriented, active	Degree of policy continuity
Interpersonal relations	Group-oriented, empathetic	Individualistic, sympathetic	Enticement tactics
Approach to conflict	Controlling, factional	Managing, coalitional	Pressure tactics
Political/ bureaucratic structure	Centralized, hierarchical, disciplined	Decentralized, collegial, weakly disciplined	Pace of decisionmaking, continuity, degree of discipline
Information management	Take in—don't give out, symbolic	Take in—give out, informative	Style of argumentation
Decision-making	Individual or bureaucratic convergence, "principled" flexibility	Consensual, compromising, functional	Style of agreement

that Mao Zedong's policies were appropriate to revolutions throughout the world; and most recently, in Beijing's efforts to speak as a leader of the nations of the Third World.

There are significant differences, however, in Chinese and American orientations to dealings with the outside world. U.S. officials approach foreign relations with the expansive and relatively optimistic perspective that has been fundamental to the American national experience. While the world presents threats and challenges, the United States—by virtue of its power and the self-confidence of its multinational population—has been able for the most part to cope successfully with and benefit from its dealings with other nations. (Exceptions are its experiences in Korea and Vietnam.) The Chinese, in contrast, approach foreign affairs from the perspective of a peasant society with a distinctive and homogeneous culture that has flourished over five millennia of continuous history as a self-contained civilization. Moreover, China's "recent" contact with the outside world—i.e., since the early 1800s—has been an experience of unsuccessful efforts to fend off unwanted foreign military and cultural intrusions, and frustrating efforts in the twentieth century to adapt its ancient culture, political order, and economy to Western practices.

What is the significance of these differences in world outlook for the negotiating process? Both Chinese and American elites assume that virtually all international political, security, and economic issues are relevant to their foreign policies, and to their bilateral dialogue. Yet the PRC lacks the power and global reach to be an active factor in most international issues, which imparts an edge of pretentiousness to discussions by PRC leaders on various global problems, a tendency to lecture and give sage advice unburdened by the responsibilities that come with a capacity to actually influence events. Nonetheless, Chinese officials assume that their country's moral and political influence has global reach, and they see the PRC as a major factor in the strategic balance because of its geographical position on the Eurasian landmass. Even though China's contemporary power is limited, they say, its weight is critical to the balance of power in Asia. And in time, they assume, the PRC will rightfully regain China's historic greatness.

At present, however, Chinese officials present a defensive and distrusting attitude to the outside world, an attitude that is a legacy of the exploitation and aggression they feel they were subjected to in decades past. This imparts a self-righteous quality to their dealings with foreign governments, particularly those that are large and influential. PRC officials assume the worst about a foreign government's motives. They interpret its interests as self-serving and illegitimate; and they feel most comfortable in posturing themselves as the natural allies of smaller, "oppressed" peoples and countries—not of the superpowers, with whom they are forced to align on a temporary basis because of the ineluctable demands of security and economic development.

Time Perspective

Chinese and Americans bring very different time perspectives to the political process. With their 5,000 years of history and the serene and unhurried persona assumed by those in authority, PRC leaders tend to view events with a long-term, historical perspective. Mao's policy of 1973 on the Taiwan issue—"I say that we can do without Taiwan for the time being, and let it come after one hundred years. Do not take matters on this world so rapidly. Why is there need to be in such great haste?" —was formulated in a time perspective designed, in part, to be acceptable to the Chinese. In contrast, Americans have little sensitivity to the lengthy rhythms of history; they are future-oriented and driven by a sense of urgency derived from notions of efficiency and progress, as well as political institutions that create the rhythm of four-year cycles of leadership authority and policy initiative.

These differences in time orientation create some of the most delicate operational tensions in the negotiating process. PRC officials tend to assume that their U.S. counterparts are anxious to reach agreement, that they are unable to sustain continuity of policy or negotiating efforts across the boundaries of different administrations, and that they are inclined to ignore the commitments of their predecessors. While the Chinese negotiator may feel he has some advantage over his American counterpart in that he can wait out a more anxious and time-driven interlocutor, he also bears the frustration of dealing with administrations that do not provide a sense of predictability and continuity of policy and personnel.

Interpersonal Relations

There are fundamental differences between American and Chinese conceptions of social relations—a situation which makes the demonstrated personal affinity of the two peoples all the more remarkable. American individualism, emotional expressiveness, and casual affability contrast sharply with the Chinese collectivist social orientation, emotional reserve, and a concept of friendship loaded with a sense of enduring mutual obligation. These differences notwithstanding, Americans and Chinese seem to readily establish interpersonal relations characterized by warmth, good humor, and mutual respect.

The influence of these social conceptions on the negotiating process is subtle and of secondary import when compared to the weight of state interests and the disciplines of official life. Yet it is worth noting, for it shapes the receptivity of both sides to blandishments and pressures. Americans, with their strong affiliative needs, seem particularly vulnerable to Chinese appeals to "old friends." As noted earlier, PRC officials are remarkably effective in maintaining official discipline in such relationships. They will obliquely appeal to the personal political interests of their American interlocutors, while submerging their own interests in the imperatives of the political collective. Where American officials try to be *sympathetic* to the concerns of their interlocutors and seek to reach a middle ground of accommodation,[3] the Chinese are *empathetic*—skillful in reading the motives and emotions of their counterparts, yet able to keep their own perspectives firmly grounded in the policy demands and personal loyalties of their own system. U.S. negotiators should be sensitized to Chinese skill in using the "old friends" theme, in which they try to personalize the negotiating process to ensnare the foreigner in the games of *guanxi*.

Approaches to Conflict

Negotiation is, of course, one approach to conflict resolution; and Chinese and Americans have very different views about

---

3. Ambassador U. Alexis Johnson observed of his approach to the U.S.-PRC exchanges at Geneva and Warsaw, "To negotiate effectively with Wang [Bingnan] I had to try to step into his shoes and see the world his way." Johnson also notes his effort to establish informal social contacts with Wang "to probe his intentions and establish closer relations in a friendly atmosphere" (Johnson, 1984, p. 1239). The instinctive American assumption is that personal goodwill and expressions of affability will facilitate agreement among nations. (See also Iklé, 1964, pp. 159–161.)

the management of political conflict. Despite Mao Zedong's efforts to institutionalize "struggle" in the PRC political process (see Solomon, 1971, pp. 3–4, 521–524; Pye, 1968), Chinese still view with alarm overt political conflict, especially among their leaders. Conflict is to be suppressed, as are political factions, even though everyone recognizes that they exist. For Americans, conflict is accepted as a normal aspect of the political process. It is institutionalized as competition bounded by the moral and legal norms of the democratic order. Parties and coalitions are accepted as normal components of the political process.

These differing attitudes toward conflict shape Chinese approaches to pressuring their negotiating counterparts and their style of reaching agreement (see below). As we elaborated in the preceding chapter, the Chinese seek to play adversaries against one another to bring pressure to bear on a negotiator or to influence political debate in an adversary's political system—a reflection of their approach to dealing with domestic political factions. They will provoke, or confront, or raise the threat of the wrath of a billion countrymen.

Most of these tactics for bringing pressure to bear on a negotiating counterpart are, of course, well known to U.S. officials; yet they are not part of the normal set of political routines or stratagems readily implemented through the institutions of U.S. foreign relations. (For example, it would be rather difficult to play adversaries in the PRC against each other, given the combination of policy and institutional inhibitions on the U.S. side and the PRC's defenses against such interference in its internal political processes—defenses lacking in the American political system.) The American approach to pressuring a negotiating counterpart has more to do with the substantive terms of the negotiation than with manipulation of the structure of the negotiating process.

Political/Bureaucratic Structures

The authoritarian character of the Chinese political culture is institutionalized in highly centralized and hierarchical political and bureaucratic structures. And despite Mao's efforts during the Cultural Revolution to decentralize the political process and weaken the power of the government bureaucracies, the political process remains highly constrained and disciplined within Marxist-Leninist party and state organizations. In contrast, the American political system is decentralized, collegial rather than authoritarian, and relatively weakly disciplined.

These contrasting structural characteristics influence in a variety of ways the processes of political decisionmaking and negotiation. In the initial phase of the normalization process, decisions were reached by the Chinese quite rapidly, as the high-level dialogue was controlled by two men, Mao Zedong and Zhou Enlai. While the Politburo was probably used to ratify Chairman Mao's approach to dealing with the United States and to approve of key documents such as the Shanghai Communiqué, the mechanics of the relationship were quite simple. It was managed expeditiously by Zhou and his closest colleagues in the Foreign Ministry.

In more recent times, as Deng Xiaoping has rebuilt the institutions of government that were shattered during Mao's Cultural Revolution, the policymaking process and the mechanics of the U.S.-PRC relationship have become increasingly bureaucratic and sluggish.

In contrast, the U.S. system of Executive Branch/congressional decisionmaking and the freewheeling American press must appear to the Chinese as complicated, unpredictable, undisciplined, and weak in policy continuity. The precise impact of these institutional differences on the negotiating process is difficult to specify, but it seems likely that the Chinese feel they are confronting a system that is changeable, difficult to influence, and unreliable—in the sense that understandings reached with one administration may either be subverted by the bureaucracy or congressional politics, or reconsidered by successive administrations. The Chinese probably are also cautious about overtly stating in private policy positions that they anticipate will appear in the press or in the memoirs of retired senior officials.

Ironically, this freewheeling quality of the American political process creates the very qualities of unpredictability and loss of control that the more disciplined Chinese seek to induce purposefully into the negotiating process to disorient or unnerve their foreign counterparts. It probably also makes them cautious about the degree of intimacy and stability they can expect in maintaining relations with the United States. Given the extent to which they base their official dealings on the cultivation of good interpersonal relations, it must be frustrating for them to have to cope with the constant turnover of American officials. Good *guanxi* is quickly dissipated as "friends" in the Foreign Service are given new assignments and political officials are replaced as a result of electoral changes.

Information Management

There are evident and striking differences in the way Chinese and Americans convey and use information in the negotiating process. The Chinese, as noted earlier, are highly symbolic in their communications, whereas the style of American information usage is very functional. This makes the Chinese inclined to resort to the loaded political gesture, to nonverbal forms of communication, and to understated or oblique phrasing that can be interpreted at several levels. They are highly reserved in giving out information, yet they are extremely skillful in drawing out their foreign counterparts—particularly outspoken Americans. They have demonstrated their effectiveness in misleading negotiating counterparts about the state of their internal politics and their foreign-policy concerns. Their pattern of communication is "take in, don't give out," in contrast to the "take in *and* give out" American style.

In some measure, these contrasting communication styles are complementary—Chinese reserve meshing with American outspokenness—yet the Chinese probably also tend to overinterpret U.S. actions that are random or intended to be taken at face value,[4] while U.S. negotiators may be insufficiently sensitive to the implicit meanings imbued in Chinese words and actions. The Chinese style of argumentation in a negotiation is also more complex than the American and is intended to influence a range of personal and political factors more than is the relatively

4. For example, Mao's misinterpretation of the intended significance of a White House reception in his conversations with Henry Kissinger on February 17–18, 1973 (discussed in Chapter Three).

functional U.S. approach, which is oriented largely toward the substantive issues under discussion.

Decisionmaking

The decisionmaking styles of the two sides and the manner in which agreements are expressed also provide evident points of contrast. The Chinese seem to have a less cumbersome mechanism for reaching political decisions than the Americans, with their complex institutional pattern of Executive Branch/congressional/mass-media checks and balances. The U.S. pattern is consensual and compromising, while the Chinese seem to base decisions either on the initiative of the senior political leadership or on a convergence of bureaucratic interests. The Chinese demonstrate flexibility in reaching agreements if their position can be justified in terms of relevant principles as well as political self-interest; the American pattern is tied less to abstract principles and more to functional and legal requirements. Reflecting these differences, the Chinese prefer political understandings expressed in formal public documents that identify common principles (while also asserting differences in political outlook); the American preference is for legalistic documents such as treaties or highly specific contractual agreements of a technical nature (as on textiles, grain trade, and civil aviation).

5

Lessons Learned

What are the implications of this study for U.S. government efforts to manage negotiating encounters with the PRC in the service of attaining American policy objectives?

Scrutable China

Of the many lessons that can be drawn from the record of U.S. dealings with the Chinese since the 1960s, perhaps the most fundamental conclusion is that Chinese negotiating behavior is not mysterious or inscrutable. Just as Zhou Enlai asserted to Henry Kissinger during their first encounter, in response to Kissinger's characterization of the PRC as "a land of mystery," renewed Sino-American contact has indeed demystified to a significant degree the country and its political process.

The record of official exchanges since the first Kissinger-Zhou meeting reveals that the Chinese seek to manage negotiations in a highly organized and regular manner, one that is readily comprehensible by foreign observers. Moreover, the tactics they employ are quite apparent, if not universal, and often can be anticipated. There is nothing unique in their negotiating behavior, although they pursue their objectives with a distinctive style, with discipline, and with determination.

The official American negotiator should thus approach his task with the realization that his Chinese counterpart will deal with him in a manner that is comprehensible and even predictable. An intellectual understanding of the Chinese approach to managing negotiations gives U.S. officials a major advantage in preventing the Chinese from gaining such control of the process that the U.S. side becomes trapped in pressures that force an outcome detrimental to American interests.

Maximizing U.S. Control over the Negotiating Process

Whether or not U.S. negotiators seek to develop countertactics as suggested in this study, there are important aspects of the negotiating process that are under their influence; and if a negotiator manages them effectively, these aspects will maximize control over negotiating encounters. Many of the following guidelines sound straightforward, if not simple-minded, but they are fundamental to effective dealings with the Chinese (as well as with other governments). Of greater concern, they are ground rules that have been frequently violated in recent years in dealings with the Chinese. Thus, a major challenge to a U.S. negotiator is to overcome the internal bureaucratic impediments and other institutional and cultural factors that constrain his or her ability to organize and conduct a negotiation in optimal fashion.

Know the substantive issues cold. PRC negotiators are well-prepared and briefed as they enter into a negotiation. They are supported by competent staff who display bureaucratic discipline and meticulous attention to detail.

Master the past negotiating record. PRC officials conducting negotiations will have full understanding and recall of the prior negotiating record, and they will not hesitate to use this to pressure a foreign counterpart.

Control of the record is a particular problem for U.S. officials, because of their relatively brief tenure in particular offices relative to their PRC counterparts. Moreover, the dissipation of the record of official U.S. negotiating exchanges with the PRC among different government agencies, presidential libraries, and other official depositories makes it particularly difficult to assemble and analyze what is now a voluminous record of tens of thousands of pages of memcoms and reporting cables. The U.S. government would be well served in its dealings with the PRC by the establishment of a central repository of the record of Sino-American negotiating exchanges, preferably one that is readable by electronic means to facilitate searches and analysis.

Present your position in a broad framework. The Chinese distrust a legalistic approach to negotiations. Their tendency to personalize the political process—to judge a counterpart official's "sincerity" on the basis of his general attitude toward China and the U.S.-PRC relationship—and their claim to be a world power lead Chinese officials to an interest in issues that may seem unrelated to the problem at hand, especially in the early phases of a negotiation. They want to be taken seriously in terms of the general relationship as well as on technical issues. Given this orientation, it is often useful to place a specific subject under discussion in a broader framework. The Chinese may find it easier to accommodate to a negotiating counterpart's position on a technical matter if they can rationalize compromise in terms of the broader relationship (as they did in their eventual acceptance of the U.S. position on a solution to the private-claims/blocked-assets issue).

Know your own bottom line. While the Chinese may in some measure improvise their way through a protracted negotiation, they initiate or enter into the process with a clear sense of what they want as the end result; and they have shown a capacity to play out the evolution of a negotiation over an extended period of time (as is evident in the records of the normalization and Taiwan arms-sales exchanges).

For this reason, as well as others noted below, it is exceptionally important for a U.S. negotiator to establish a bottom line at the outset of a series of exchanges.

Clear understanding of one's own objectives will also help a negotiator to resist raising expectations and to assess the pitfalls in the Chinese preference for vaguely worded agreements, as well as their tendency to reserve position on issues where they are unable to obtain their objectives.

Be patient, and don't get trapped in time deadlines. PRC negotiators view time as one of their major weapons in a negotiation. They distrust quick deals and prefer extended exploration of issues, because it enables them to draw out their interlocutor before formulating their own response. Thus, anticipate the "our guest always speaks first" routine and do not expect to hear a full presentation of the PRC position until late in a series of exchanges. Moreover, the Chinese will protract a negotiation to test the resolve of their counterparts and to assess their commitment to the relationship, and they will pace exchanges until the most opportune context for the end-game phase.

This Chinese use of time contrasts sharply with the American preference for expeditious problem-solving and efficient use of time. A U.S. official should avoid negotiating under time deadlines that cannot be controlled, as the Chinese will assume that the American is more inclined to compromise when making decisions under time pressure. The U.S. negotiator should also be aware of the Chinese tendency to wait until the very last minute to conclude an agreement on the expectation that a counterpart's interest in concluding a deal will lead him or her to compromise when faced with an imminent deadline. It also helps to know that for all the Chinese posturing about their "patience," the record shows that they, too, are vulnerable to time pressures when negotiating under a deadline. The best protection against such pressures, of course, is the willingness to walk away from a negotiation when it seems to be going nowhere or when a deal seems unfavorable, despite an approaching deadline.

The need for bureaucratic and political discipline. Given the Chinese propensity to look for and exploit political and bureaucratic rivalries in counterpart governments, it is necessary to take measures to ensure a unified policy position and an implementive approach to dealing with the PRC. The friendship game can be turned against the Chinese (as was suggested in the preceding chapter), but to do so, the presumed rivals on the U.S. side must be conscious of the Chinese ploy and willing to cooperate in response to it. And in view of the tendency of the Chinese to look for friendly interlocutors in various government agencies, policy toward the PRC must be coordinated on an interagency basis.

Minimize media pressures. The Chinese will try to use media visibility to bring pressures to bear on a counterpart government; therefore, negotiations are best controlled when carried out in confidence. Moreover, the Chinese view a confidential approach to managing a negotiation as a measure of their counterpart's seriousness of purpose.

The Chinese use their own media to try to set a negotiating agenda and to create the impression of inflexibility on certain principles and positions. The U.S. negotiator should resist any inclination to accept publicly communicated policy positions as Beijing's negotiating framework. Moreover, while the Chinese have not hesitated to criticize U.S. policies in the PRC mass media, it is counterproductive to the relationship to polemicize via the press. Experience has shown that the Chinese can be shamed for posturing for the media.

Analyze the PRC internal political context and the negotiating style of the official interlocutors. The record shows clearly that China's internal politics have had a significant effect on PRC negotiating behavior. Leadership feuds have their impact on foreign relations, and the flexibility of Beijing's negotiators is influenced by the degree of dissension in the leadership and the power of the senior figure. Moreover, the Chinese have attempted to control the timing of negotiations to mesh with the workings of their internal political processes (this was particularly notable in the Taiwan arms-sales negotiation).

The problem for the foreign negotiator, of course, is that the ability of outsiders to assess the state of the PRC domestic political scene is at best limited. We usually understand clearly the political forces at play only in retrospect, and such hindsight is of limited value in conducting future negotiations. Perhaps the most useful conclusion that can be drawn, apart from the need to improve our efforts at "Beijingology," is that PRC rigidity or polemicizing across the negotiating table is usually a sign of leadership conflict, and in this situation the political environment is not propitious for reaching agreement if PRC accommodation is required. At such times, an aloof stance is likely to be more effective than one of pressing the Chinese for demonstrations of flexibility they may not be able to give.

It is also important for the foreign official to understand as much as possible about the background, personality, and negotiating style of his PRC counterpart. This is no easy task, for the Chinese try to keep such aspects of their internal circumstances obscure to foreigners. Yet given the degree to which they personalize the negotiating process, it is useful, even as background information, to understand the attitudes and style of the Chinese officials managing a negotiation, their interpersonal relations, and their associations with more senior figures in the leadership.

Develop a negotiating strategy and apply tactics to counter Chinese negotiating ploys. PRC officials are not superhuman in their capacity to manage a negotiation to their country's advantage; yet the combination of bureaucratic centralization, political discipline, and a culturally ingrained sense of the use of stratagems to compensate for vulnerabilities in dealing with more powerful foreigners makes their approach to negotiating highly purposeful, controlled, and "gamed out." They will enter into a negotiation with a clear sense of objectives, an overall strategy, and a willingness to use tactical ploys to enmesh a counterpart official in a relationship and a process within which he can be exposed to blandishments and pressures intended to foster the attainment of PRC objectives.

A U.S. negotiator should *not* assume that his Chinese counterpart is improvising his approach to official encounters, just as he should not assume that PRC officials are uniquely crafty, in total control, or invulnerable to the same enticements and pressures they seek to impose on their adversaries.

The best strategy in negotiating with the Chinese—beyond effective management of the aspects of the process that are under American control—is to enter into a series of exchanges with a broad game plan, a clear set of goals, and a willingness to make tactical moves (in part in response to Chinese manipulations) designed to demonstrate competence and control over the negotiating process.

The most effective posture for dealing with the Chinese is one neither of domination nor of supplication (which the Chinese are quite effective in evoking from foreigners), but rather an attitude of restrained openness, of willingness to search for common interests while recognizing the many significant differences between the two countries. At the same time, a U.S. capacity to counter the more egregious Chinese tactical manipulations will communicate to PRC officials a sense of competence and control and a determination to negotiate in the service of defending and enhancing U.S. interests.

PART TWO

Chinese Negotiating Behavior Revisited

Chas. W. Freeman, Jr.

Enormous changes have taken place both in China and in Chinese relations with the international community since Richard Solomon wrote this seminal study of the Chinese national negotiating style, based on the experience of American negotiators with the Beijing leadership in the 1970s. For much of the 1970s, mainland China was very isolated, in the last days of Chairman Mao's totalitarian dictatorship, and struggling to emerge from the chaos of his supremely idiosyncratic and destructive "Great Proletarian Cultural Revolution." Through the middle of the decade, the Chinese government and its diplomacy were under the close personal supervision of Premier Zhou Enlai, a man universally regarded as remarkable for his leadership skills, diplomatic craft, and urbane cosmopolitanism. As the 1970s ended, a formidably pragmatic new leader, Deng Xiaoping, set China on a long counter-march away from the xenophobia, ideological introversion, and statist economics that had been the common heritage of Soviet and Chinese communism.

At the outset of the decade upon most of which Ambassador Solomon's research was based, China's seat in the United Nations was still held by Taipei, and Beijing had only the most tenuous of dialogues with Washington. By its end, the People's Republic of China had emerged as a respected, if still fairly passive, permanent member of the UN Security Council. The United States had, to the initial surprise of both countries, become China's most influential international connection. Even by the standards of China's tumultuous modern history, the frequency, speed, and thoroughness with which the political winds shifted in the 1970s were exceptional.

This unusual decade would have seemed unlikely to yield conclusions of lasting validity about Chinese negotiating behavior; all the less likely, given the stunning advances in Chinese sophistication about the outside world that twenty subsequent years of unprecedented receptivity to foreign influences brought about. China has changed in astonishing ways over the past fifteen and more years. The subjects on which China negotiated internationally in the 1970s were limited almost entirely to the realm of bilateral relations (especially the establishment of diplomatic relations with foreign states) and to political, diplomatic, and consular subjects. Since then, the subjects and contexts in which Chinese negotiate have expanded to embrace all of the political, economic, military, and cultural topics of concern to the international community.

Yet, fifteen years after the Solomon analysis was first published as a classified document, his conclusions have lost none of their force and utility. He succeeded brilliantly, on the basis of much less experience and information than are available to us now, in capturing the durable essence of China's distinctive national negotiating style. With respect to the fundamentals of the Chinese negotiating practices he describes, in fact, it seems fair to say: *plus ça change, plus c'est la même chose.*

As they negotiate, Chinese officials and business representatives continue to see their task as establishing or extending personal relationships, as well as working out the details of particular transactions, with foreigners. Chinese negotiators therefore still place greater stress than most of their foreign counterparts on gaining a shared commitment to certain "principles" (the strategic or basic understandings that will guide interaction on key issues over the long term). Once the possibility of a long-term relationship has been determined, Chinese negotiators will emphasize the need to search for common ground on specific issues, while reserving seemingly irreconcilable differences for later resolution. In their view, this approach *(qiu tong cun yi)* allows common interests gradually to outweigh points in contention and fosters the growth of mutual trust. It thus holds in reserve a basis for the ultimate resolution of issues that are currently intractable.

In commercial negotiations, the emphasis on defining relationships broadly and then making them work in specific cases means Chinese negotiators can be easily put off by the attempts of Western lawyers to define in detail how contractual arrangements will work before they have even begun. For many Chinese businesspersons, a contract resembles a prenuptial agreement. It defines who will get what if the marriage breaks down. It should not attempt to regulate daily interaction within the marriage. For contracts, as for marriage, in this Chinese view, both parties should understand that if it becomes necessary to refer to the details and documentation of their agreement in order to solve problems in their relationship, then their relationship is on its way to breaking down.

The Chinese emphasis on agreements in principle to be followed by continuously negotiated practical arrangements for implementation can be broadly successful in the right context. This is well illustrated by the remarkable improvements in China's post–Cold War relations with Russia, the newly independent Central Asian states, the Republic of Korea (ROK), and Vietnam. That this Chinese approach can succeed despite efforts by one or both sides to reinterpret what has been previously agreed upon can be seen in the ultimately uneventful British return of Hong Kong to Chinese sovereignty. That it can fail when common understandings on "principles" or mutual sincerity about developing a relationship are lacking is shown in the sudden about-face in Sino-Indian relations in 1998 following India's nuclear weapons tests and India's accompanying declarations about the extent of its distrust and hostility toward China. That an approach based on agreement in principle, the search for common interests, and deferral of difficult issues for later resolution can register only uncertain success is evident in the many twists and turns of Sino-American relations over the Taiwan question as well as in cross-Strait relations themselves.

No Chinese statesman would agree with Napoleon's belittling of the importance of agreements in principle: "principles are fine; they entail no commitment."[1] If forced to draw up a balance sheet on their nation's diplomacy, however, Chinese statesmen might well now lament that "agreement in principle may mean disagreement in practice."[2] Nonetheless, there is no substantial evidence that Chinese negotiators have felt obliged to reassess or change their basic approach to dealing with their foreign counterparts. Their approach to negotiation remains very much as Ambassador Solomon has described it.

This is so despite the fact that, with the benefit of a decade or two of my own interchanges with Chinese colleagues, some of China's negotiating preferences now look a bit less like considered judgments about how to manipulate foreign counterparts and a bit more like pragmatic accommodations to practical difficulties. Chinese negotiators have faced budgetary constraints, problems born of the imperative of adhering to ideologically mandated stands ("political correctness"), bureaucratic rigidities, inefficient communications technology, and intelligence gaps. These problems are hardly unique to Chinese negotiators (although the *combination* of all of them may be *sui generis*). Nevertheless, as Chinese negotiators made a virtue of necessity, these problems probably helped them evolve the distinctive national style that Solomon first identified. Practical considerations as well as cultural predilections have tended to reinforce each other.

For example, foreign exchange limitations long constrained foreign travel by Chinese officials. This had a big impact on their willingness to conduct negotiations outside China. (One notorious instance of such official parsimony occurred during Vice Premier Deng Xiaoping's first visit to the United Nations General

---

1. Cited in Chas. W. Freeman, Jr., *The Diplomat's Dictionary*, revised edition, Washington, D.C.: United States Institute of Peace Press, 1997, p. 233.

2. Ibid., p. 234.

Assembly, in 1974. Deng was authorized a total of U.S. $10 for his personal use. His staff had the difficult task of breaking the news to him that this would not buy very much in terms of gifts for his grandchildren.) Not until the mid-1980s did Chinese diplomats begin to be authorized to spend official funds in foreign currency for entertainment outside embassy or other official premises. It is thus not unimportant to recognize that the Chinese preference for dealing with foreigners on their own ground was reinforced by fiscal stringencies.

Similarly, given the harsh penalties for any apparent tendency to question the rectitude of official positions—and the reasoning on which these positions rest—that the Chinese political system could at times mete out, Chinese diplomats have had to be especially cautious in their efforts to state or explain the policies of foreign states to their leaders. They cannot appear to be in sympathy with foreign views.[3] To have a reputation for "clientitis" in his own capital is a severe liability for any negotiator. In China, at various points in the past, such an image could literally be fatal. In any event, unless foreigners can be made to state their negotiating positions in their own words for the Chinese record, Chinese officials have found it difficult to state these positions for them as they help their leaders formulate judgments about what it may be possible actually to achieve in negotiations. Thus the political culture has inclined Chinese diplomats to prefer to have foreign negotiators state their views first. The record that the foreign negotiating team establishes provides an objective basis for their Chinese counterparts to validate their negotiating instructions with their superiors. (Waiting till one hears the actual position of a foreign negotiator always has the merit, in any event, of avoiding the problem of "negotiating with oneself," that is, formulating negotiating instructions on

3. "Statesmen value the expertise of diplomats in part because diplomats understand and can explain the actions and motivations of foreign states. But it is difficult to explain actions and motivations without seeming to justify or sympathize with them. Diplomats easily come to be seen as too solicitous of the interests of foreign states and insufficiently devoted to the interests of their own. They must temper their remarks to preclude this perception or lose the ear of policymakers." Chas. W. Freeman, Jr., *Arts of Power: Statecraft and Diplomacy,* Washington, D.C.: United States Institute of Peace Press, 1997, p. 130.

the basis of perhaps ill-founded conjecture about what may or may not be acceptable to the other side.)

Chinese negotiators are, of course, far from unusual in wishing to have their counterparts speak first. It is sound negotiating practice under most circumstances to ask that one's opponent reveal his position—perhaps foreshadowing concessions he may be prepared to make—before one begins to lay out one's own stand at the negotiating table. Even when previous meetings have occurred, and a full record of a foreign negotiating position has been established, it remains advantageous to maneuver an opponent into showing as much of his bargaining hand as he can be induced to reveal. Admittedly, however, Chinese negotiators carry this consideration to an extreme in their unabashedly contradictory statements in China that "the guest should speak first" and abroad that "the host should speak first."

Chinese managers are notoriously chary about delegation of authority. They are famous for micromanaging, nit-picking, and second-guessing. This has been a particular problem for negotiators representing the Chinese government abroad. Both they and their decisionmaking superiors are much more comfortable being in direct physical contact with each other than they are with situations in which they must communicate electronically, that is, guardedly and obliquely. (Chinese are far from unique in preferring a short chain of command as they maneuver at the negotiating table.) The relatively primitive and slow communications technology available to Chinese negotiators in the past gave them an added reason to stay close to Zhongnanhai. In recent years Chinese communications systems have been greatly upgraded, but negotiating in China still helps Chinese negotiators obtain speedier and more authoritative guidance from their superiors. This further reinforces their tendency to prefer negotiating venues in China to those abroad.

Intelligence considerations have been another factor causing Chinese to favor negotiating on their home ground. There are obvious informational advantages to having a foreign leader or negotiator in Beijing, where his interactions with his subordinates can often be overheard and his attitudes plumbed by protocol officers and interpreters who accompany him on sightseeing excursions. This was especially important in the past, when China was relatively isolated and lacked understanding of the influences of interest-group politics and other constraints on foreign negotiating positions. In the absence of reliable and direct sources of information, much Chinese intelligence analysis then relied on a combination of press reporting and *a priori* reasoning. The flow of raw intelligence directly to leaders while they actually engaged in interaction with a foreign leader or negotiator in Beijing could often be a healthy corrective to mistaken presuppositions.

In fact, one of the most notable changes in Chinese negotiating behavior is in the area of intelligence gathering.[4] Chinese politics is far less stressful and constraining today than in the era of Chairman Mao and the Gang of Four. Chinese diplomatic and intelligence reporting is, by all accounts, much more honest and less likely to be trimmed to fit the political winds than in revolutionary times or an era of intense leadership conflict. China's opening to the outside world has also greatly improved its intellectuals' understanding of foreign societies, even as it has helped foreigners to find the Chinese less exotic. Chinese analysts have climbed a steep learning curve over the past decade. They are far better versed in the nature, dynamics, and details of politics in democratic societies than anyone in China was when it was still a relatively isolated country that viewed the world through the distorting lenses of Marxism–Leninism–Mao Zedong thought. China's long and distinguished traditions of scholarship are blossoming into an increasingly diverse and ever higher quality Chinese-language literature on foreign affairs.

Chinese think tanks, whether official or only loosely related to the government, have mushroomed in recent years. These research outfits have rapidly developed their own wide networks of contacts abroad. Many Chinese researchers now have easy access to their counterparts in foreign societies and, indeed, to foreign government offices and officials. For China, as for Japan, it is now

4. "Intelligence is knowledge that is relevant to statecraft." Ibid., p. 23.

standard practice that think tanks dispatch a small horde of scholars, policy analysts, and researchers abroad on intelligence-gathering missions in advance of summit meetings or other major encounters of Chinese leaders with foreign counterparts. These specialists meet with their foreign counterparts, contacts, and friends, take the pulse of politics in the foreign country or countries concerned, and then write confidential reports and policy recommendations for the leadership.

China's current leaders are also better equipped to make effective use of such material than their predecessors. They are better educated, at home with Western notions of political economy, and more at ease in international settings. (President Jiang Zemin participates regularly in APEC and other multilateral gatherings at the level of chief of government. Premier Zhu Rongji and several of his immediate subordinates in China's State Council have become fixtures at the annual conclaves of the world's tycoons and their straphangers in the "World Economic Forum" at Davos.)

A surprising number of senior officials in China today speak English (or another foreign language). Recently Chinese leaders have even begun to practice a rudimentary form of public diplomacy. They now occasionally hold press conferences that are televised both in China and abroad, despite the potential for political embarrassment that such unstructured encounters with the Western press entail.[5] The Chinese Ministry of Foreign Affairs now has daily press briefings at which it issues (often peculiarly worded but moderately informative) statements, clarifications, and denials.

Beijing remains at a severe disadvantage, however, in the realm of public diplomacy in this age of democracy. China remains under the rule of a monopoly political movement, the Chinese Communist Party (CCP), dedicated to maintaining a Leninist system of one-party political control. The press in the People's

---

5. Note the remark by Harold Macmillan that "a Foreign Secretary . . . is always faced with this cruel dilemma. Nothing he can say can do very much good, and almost anything he may say may do a great deal of harm. Anything he says that is not obvious is dangerous; whatever is not trite is risky. He is forever poised between the cliché and the indiscretion." Cited in *The Diplomat's Dictionary*, p. 254.

Republic is now more diverse, vigorous, and engaged in investigative journalism than ever before. It remains, however, in most respects a captive organ of the CCP. Restrictions on the activities of foreign journalists resident in China, and their harassment by Chinese security organs, guarantee that even those most inclined to give China the benefit of the doubt are driven to alienation and hostility soon after their arrival. China will suffer from a very bad foreign press that will complicate the ability of its negotiators to achieve their nation's international objectives for as long as this remains the case.

Moreover, despite significant evolution in the functions and importance of the National People's Congress (NPC) as the role of law expands in Chinese society, NPC members are not yet true counterparts of Western legislators and cannot deal with them as such. The current era is one in which national legislatures play a much more direct and independent role in foreign affairs, including on many issues of concern to China, than was the case in the past. The Chinese Foreign Ministry has recognized this and is attempting to improve outreach to foreign legislators by its diplomats. (The Chinese embassy in Washington, for example, now has a growing staff devoted to the cultivation of relations with the U.S. Congress.) But the highly structured and often stilted style of diplomatic discourse and démarches is ill suited to dialogue with legislators. China is having a hard time developing effective communication with them. In the absence of such rapport, however, foreign legislators will continue to be poorly informed and skeptical, if not hostile, to Chinese positions on matters of concern to them.

As of the end of the twentieth century, in short, China remains conspicuous by its failure to develop many of the tools of diplomacy that other nations consider essential to support the work of their negotiators abroad, such as effective outreach to legislators, interest groups, and the concerned public. Such aspects of contemporary diplomacy are essential to arming a negotiator with the ability to influence foreign negotiating positions as they are being formed. Such public diplomacy can ensure that the negotiator is well informed about the underlying concerns and motivations of a foreign government before negotiations begin. It can give him a sense of where the hard and soft positions in the opposing negotiator's strategy may lie. Public diplomacy can channel different messages to different interest groups abroad. It can help a negotiator undercut backing for the opposite side's instructions by its government, its legislature, and even its people. Many foreign ministries and embassies, lacking the in-house skills or staffing to support their negotiators in this way, engage the services of public relations firms or lobbyists, at least until they can develop an in-house capability. China has yet to do so. (This is by marked—and somewhat surprising—contrast with Chinese in Taiwan, who are widely acknowledged to be among the world's most skilled practitioners of the arts of public and government relations.)

The relative incapacity of Chinese negotiators to influence or understand the inner history of foreign negotiating positions before they harden into approved instructions reinforces some of the elements of their negotiating style that Richard Solomon analyzed based on the experience of the 1970s. These include their desire to separate foreign negotiators from their domestic context by meeting on Chinese ground, and their insistence on hearing the foreign negotiator's position before stating their own. Lack of support from public diplomacy also leaves Chinese negotiators at a distinct disadvantage, especially in the case of negotiations that are well publicized and not very confidential. (Examples include negotiations over trade issues, as well as the discussions on various aspects of cross-strait relations between Taipei and Beijing.) China remains a relatively poor performer in the arena of press relations, for all the reasons discussed above.

As China has been drawn into the existing world order, it has found itself increasingly engaged in the "parliamentary diplomacy" of multilateral organizations, often on highly technical subjects. Chinese participation in these organizations has followed an admirably consistent pattern. For the first few years of China's membership, its representatives have tended to be relatively passive, as they strive—patiently and meticulously—to master subject matters and procedures peculiar to each organization. In time, however, they begin to rise from the backbenches. (Organizational improvements in the Chinese foreign ministry and the modernization of Chinese diplomatic communications systems now enable Chinese diplomats to respond on a more timely basis to approaches from their foreign colleagues than was the case in the early years after Beijing's 1971 entry into the United Nations system.) In multilateral contexts, as in others, Chinese negotiators often seem to give special attention to the cultivation of long-term relationships, showing a willingness to make tactical sacrifices in order to avoid giving offense in the interest of achieving longer-term strategic gains in relations with other member states. Still, in international and transnational organizations, even if its representatives often seem to be both more deferential to international consensus and on a tighter leash than those of other great powers, China now plays the game much as other nations do.

The post–Cold War period has also seen the United States and other countries begin to insist that China conform its domestic policies and laws to generally accepted international standards as a precondition for normal political and economic relationships. (As distasteful as the Chinese have found this focus on features of their domestic system that foreigners find objectionable, they have been surprisingly pragmatic in responding to it, recognizing the need to do so as the price for developing international relationships they value.) One example of such a domestically focused negotiation is the on-again, off-again Sino-American dialogue about the treatment of dissidents and minorities, as well as other human rights developments in China that distress ordinary Americans and their representatives in Congress. Others are the Sino-American confrontations over intellectual property rights and export controls on militarily sensitive technology that erupted from time to time throughout the early and mid-1990s. In such cases, China has often found itself negotiating, in effect, with the U.S. Congress through the medium of the American executive branch of government. Negotiations of this sort are, as noted, something that China is poorly equipped to manage with its traditional approach to diplomacy.

China's rapid march toward restored wealth and power, especially since the late Deng Xiaoping's 1992 "southern tour" kicked off a new cycle of even more vigorous economic advance in the country, has raised China's international profile and levied new demands on it. There is a growing range of issues, from the health of the Asian and world economies, to the environment and global warming, control of undesirable missile technology transfers, the authorization and conduct of international peacekeeping operations, and so forth that the global community cannot address without China's cooperation. Meanwhile, the Chinese military's shows of force in the Taiwan Strait in 1995–96, intended to deter movement toward separatism and possible "independence" by Taiwanese politicians, raised new concerns. As a result of international apprehensions about possible Chinese assertiveness in the coming century, a virtual international industry devoted to conjecture about Beijing's future territorial aspirations and military behavior has come into being.

The diversity of the subject matters with which China must deal, now that it is broadly engaged in the world, has—as elsewhere—had the effect of undermining its Foreign Ministry's capability to coordinate and control dealings with foreign governments and their representatives. A widening circle of ministries and other governmental bodies has been drawn into direct relationships and negotiations with foreign counterparts. China's Ministry of Foreign Trade and Economic Cooperation (MOFTEC) has had the lead on the long-running negotiations for Chinese entry into the GATT and its successor, the World Trade Organization (WTO). MOFTEC has not been especially deferential to the Foreign Ministry. Human rights issues engage the ministries of Public Security, State Security, Justice, Civil Affairs, and others, including Chinese provincial authorities, in dialogue with foreign negotiators. Intellectual property issues bring in all of these and others.

Even within the People's Liberation Army (PLA), traditionally one of the most inward focused of the world's armed forces, military officials have found it necessary to initiate international contacts and diplomacy. The PLA now participates in negotiations about nuclear and missile proliferation issues, for example. Senior PLA officers conduct dialogues with a widening range of foreign counterparts, even as more junior officers negotiate contracts for the international purchase or sale of major defense equipment. China, like the United States and major West European nations, now practices "cooperative engagement" with foreign militaries, intended to reassure them of its benign intentions and limited capabilities. Prior to its withdrawal from most such business activities in 1998, the PLA's need to supplement its meager budget with profits from military-operated industries also required it to negotiate with a widening circle of businesses abroad. These negotiations drew the PLA out of its isolation and helped it to become less xenophobic and more sophisticated in considering foreign viewpoints.

The increasing openness of Chinese politics and the growing complexity of the Chinese economy have meanwhile infected China with the virus of bureaucratic and interest-group politics. China is a long way from having anything like the lobbyists who infest Capitol Hill in Washington, but it has a bureaucratic-industrial complex that is quick to defend its vested interests when it sees these as in danger of being compromised in negotiation with foreigners. This accounts for much of the difficulty China has had in coming to grips with the terms of entry into the WTO that the United States and other industrialized countries have demanded. It also is a measure of the extent to which Chinese exceptionalism is eroding as China assimilates itself into the global economic and political systems.

Here it is worth noting a continuing organizational peculiarity of the Chinese foreign ministry and defense establishment. Chinese diplomats, military staff officers, and bureaucrats tend to specialize in their careers to a greater extent and for much longer periods than is normal in other countries. Those who deal with foreign affairs may spend their entire career dealing with a particular country or region without rotating into assignments dealing with other areas. This means that they have a formidable command of the history and record of bilateral relations with the country or countries on which they have specialized. It also means that, unless and until some systematic program of rotation between areas and functions is established, Chinese diplomats and bureaucrats will have limited breadth and familiarity with issues remote from the bilateral or organizational interactions on which they are expert. (In China, it is still expected that policy integration will be done directly by the country's most senior leaders rather than in councils below them.)

As specialists on particular foreign relationships, Chinese officials tend to develop close familiarity with the cultural peculiarities and national negotiating styles of those foreigners with whom they have dealt over the years. Inevitably, as they learn what works best with foreign counterparts, their own approach to negotiations is affected. Each bilateral or organizational relationship tends in time to develop its own subculture and its own distinctive sub-style of negotiation. In the past, this tendency was reinforced by the absence of any retirement age for Chinese officials. This meant that, in some cases, the same official would be in charge of a function for decades and in a position to put his personal stamp on the way in which it was managed. There is now a great deal more staff turnover in Chinese bureaucracies than there used to be. However, the established bureaucratic norms and negotiating traditions seem to be effectively transmitted from seniors to juniors through mentoring and on-the-job tutoring.

China's America specialists seem, for example, to approach international bargaining differently than its experts on Japan or the United Nations. As Chinese have become heavily engaged in commercial transactions with the United States, they have apparently come to expect that American counterparts will use the "salami tactics" that Henry Kissinger saw as so refreshingly absent from the Chinese negotiating style he encountered in the early 1970s. Chinese accustomed to negotiating with the United States have now concluded, on the basis of years of experience, however, that most Americans expect to reach agreement at a price or on terms roughly midway between those asked and those offered. These Chinese negotiators have learned to adjust their own expectations and approaches accordingly. They have gotten pretty good at salami-slicing themselves. But discussions with Japanese colleagues in the Gaimusho suggest that the Chinese diplomats they routinely deal with have learned to take approaches that are more congenial and more effective with Japanese than this. And, as noted, Chinese have learned to play the game at the United Nations and in other international fora as others do, and with increasing effectiveness. As China has stepped out into the world, therefore, its negotiating behavior has adapted, becoming more like that of foreign counterparts and less obviously distinctive.

The emergence of negotiating "sub-styles" illustrates the extent to which Chinese diplomats have developed the ability to deal more effectively with their foreign counterparts by learning these counterparts' national negotiating styles and adjusting their own styles to match them. Not all Chinese negotiators are such area- or organization-specializing diplomats, however, and even when they are, their approach to negotiations ultimately derives from a broader, Chinese tradition of negotiation. In this respect, it is hard to overestimate the utility of the insight that

> *There* are *distinct and repetitive patterns in Chinese negotiating behavior, and [foreign] negotiators should draw confidence from the fact that their [Chinese] counterparts will conduct negotiations in a relatively predictable manner, one that has been dealt with effectively by other [foreign] officials in pursuit of [their nation's] policy objectives.*

Time has validated these judgments by Ambassador Solomon and underscored the value of his recommendations for American and other foreign negotiators seeking to prepare themselves to deal with Chinese counterparts.

As China has become more engaged internationally and grown in wealth and power, the frequency with which foreigners have been drawn into negotiation with Chinese has increased apace. This underscores both the importance of understanding and learning to cope with the distinctive Chinese negotiating style and the value of the analytical work that Richard Solomon initiated in the 1980s. Chinese negotiators have added new elements to their style, even as they have remained true to their traditions while China has undergone changes of breathtaking intensity and scale. Fortunately, both scholars and practitioners are now publishing a growing number of case studies and histories of negotiations with the Chinese. These could form the basis of further studies that would update and expand the work that Solomon pioneered.

Beyond the extent to which it illuminated the case of China itself, perhaps the most lasting and significant insight of Richard Solomon's work is that virtually all countries display certain distinctive qualities in their negotiating behaviors, that these characteristics—derivative of the society's history and culture (as well as practical constraints)—can be analyzed systematically, and that lessons for negotiators can be drawn from such analysis. His book on Chinese negotiating behavior can serve as a template for the identification and study of other national negotiating styles, especially those of nations that do not share the heritage of European civilization. Many expect that in the coming century, the world's economic center of gravity will shift, for the first time in half a millennium, away from Europe and the Atlantic community toward East and South Asia. Understanding the ways in which the nations of that and other regions beyond Europe negotiate will be key to advancing the national interests of the United States and many other nations allied with us.

Bibliography

This updated bibliography includes all the entries from the original edition plus numerous new entries that bring the story up to the present.

Chinese Politics, Negotiations, and Sino-U.S. Relations

Beam, Jacob D. *Multiple Exposure: An American Ambassador's Unique Perspective on East-West Issues*. New York: W.W. Norton, 1978.

Blackman, Carolyn. *Negotiating China: Case Studies and Strategies*. St. Leonards, Australia: Allen & Unwin, 1997.

Brown, Roger G. "Chinese Politics and American Policy: A New Look at the Triangle." *Foreign Policy,* No. 23, Summer 1976.

Brzezinski, Zbigniew. *Power and Principle: Memoirs of the National Security Advisor, 1977–1981*. New York: Farrar, Straus, Giroux, 1983.

Burr, William, ed. *The Kissinger Transcripts: The Top Secret Talks with Beijing and Moscow*. New York: New Press, 1999.

Bush, George, and Brent Scowcroft. *A World Transformed*. New York: Knopf, 1998.

Cabot, John Moors. *First Line of Defense: Forty Years' Experiences of a Career Diplomat*. Washington, D.C.: Georgetown University, 1979.

Carter, Jimmy. *Keeping Faith: Memoirs of a President*. New York: Bantam Books, 1982.

Chang, Parris H. "Mao's Last Stand." *Problems of Communism,* Vol. 25, No. 4, July–August 1976.

——. "Interview with Hu Yaobang." *Problems of Communism,* Vol. 32, No. 6, November–December 1983.

Chen, Goh Bee. *Negotiating with the Chinese.* Aldershot, U.K.: Dartmouth Publishing Company, 1996.

Chen, Zhenxiong. "Loyalty to Supervisor, Organizational Commitment, and Employee Outcome: The Chinese Case." Ph.D. thesis. Hong Kong: Hong Kong University of Science and Technology, 1997.

Cohen, Jerome A. *Contract Laws of the People's Republic of China.* Chicago, Ill.: Longman Group (Far East) Ltd., 1988.

Dean, Arthur H. "Negotiating with the Chinese." *New York Times Magazine,* October 30, 1966.

Deng Xiaoping. "Report on the Current Situation and Our Tasks." January 16, 1980, translated in *Foreign Broadcast Information Service, PRC Supplement,* March 11, 1980, pp. 1–27.

DePauw, John W. *U.S.-Chinese Trade Negotiations.* New York: Praeger, 1981.

Dittmer, Lowell. "Chinese Informal Politics." *China Journal,* July 1995, pp. 1–24.

Dong, Lisheng, ed. *Administrative Reform in the People's Republic of China Since 1978.* Working Papers Series No. 1. Leiden: International Institute for Asian Studies, 1994.

Eastman, Lloyd E. *Throne and Mandarins: China's Search for a Policy During the Sino-French Controversy, 1880–1885.* Cambridge, Mass.: Harvard University Press, 1967.

Fairbank, John K., and Teng, Ssu-yu. *China's Response to the West: A Documentary Survey, 1839–1923.* Cambridge, Mass.: Harvard University Press, 1954.

Foot, Rosemary. *The Practice of Power: U.S. Relations with China since 1949.* New York: Oxford University Press, 1997.

Freeman, Charles W., Jr. "Notes on the Chinese Negotiating Style." Unpublished paper prepared for East Asian Legal Studies, Harvard Law School, 1975.

Fried, Morton H. *The Fabric of Chinese Society.* New York: Octagon, 1969.

Haig, Alexander M. *Caveat: Realism, Reagan, and Foreign Policy.* New York: Macmillan, 1984.

Hersh, Seymour M. *The Price of Power: Kissinger in the Nixon White House.* New York: Summit, 1983.

Holdridge, John H. *Crossing the Divide: An Insider's Account of the Normalization of U.S.-China Relations.* Lanham, Md.: Rowman and Littlefield, 1997.

Hsu, Immanuel C. Y. *China's Entrance into the Family of Nations: The Diplomatic Phase, 1858–1880*. Cambridge, Mass.: Harvard University Press, 1960.

Hunt, Michael H. *The Genesis of Chinese Communist Foreign Policy*. New York: Columbia University Press, 1996.

Johnson, U. Alexis. *The Right Hand of Power: The Memoirs of an American Diplomat*. Englewood Cliffs, N.J.: Prentice-Hall, 1984.

Johnston, Alastair. *Cultural Realism: Strategic Culture and Grand Strategy in Chinese History*. Princeton: Princeton University Press, 1995.

Joy, C. Turner. *How Communists Negotiate*. New York: Macmillan, 1955.

Kissinger, Henry. *White House Years*. Boston: Little, Brown, 1979.

——. *Years of Upheaval*. Boston: Little, Brown, 1982.

——. *Diplomacy*. New York: Simon and Schuster, 1994.

Kuan, John C. *The KMT-CCP Wartime Negotiations, 1937–1945*. Taipei: The Asia and World Institute, 1982.

Kuriyama, Takakazu. "Some Legal Aspects of the Japan-China Joint Communiqué." *Japanese Annual of International Law,* 1973, pp. 42–51.

Lall, Arthur. *How Communist China Negotiates*. New York: Columbia University Press, 1968.

Lardy, Nicholas R. *China in the World Economy*. Washington, D.C.: Institute for International Economics, 1994.

Li, Wei. *The Chinese Staff System: A Mechanism for Bureaucratic Control and Integration*. China Research Monograph No. 44. Berkeley, Calif.: Institute of East Asian Studies, University of California, 1994.

Li Zhisui. *The Private Life of Chairman Mao*. New York: Random House, 1995.

Liberthal, Kenneth. "The Foreign Policy Debate in Peking as Seen Through Allegorical Articles, 1973–76." *China Quarterly,* No. 71, September 1977, pp. 528–544.

——. *Governing China: From Revolution Through Reform*. New York: W.W. Norton, 1995.

Lieberthal, Kenneth G., and David M. Lampton, eds. *Bureaucracy, Politics, and Decision Making in Post-Mao China*. Berkeley, Calif.: University of California Press, 1992.

Lifton, Robert J. *Thought Reform and the Psychology of Totalism*. New York: Norton, 1963.

——. *Revolutionary Immortality: Mao Tse-tung and the Chinese Cultural Revolution*. New York: Random House, 1968.

Lu, Ning. *The Dynamics of Foreign-Policy Decisionmaking in China.* Boulder, Colo.: Westview Press, 1997.

Lu Yuan. "Those Who Show No Understanding of the Times Will Surely Meet with a Rebuff." *People's Daily*, in *Foreign Broadcast Information Service, PRC,* December 9, 1980.

MacFarquhar, Roderick. *The Origins of the Cultural Revolution. Vol. 3: The Coming of the Cataclysm, 1961–1966.* New York: Columbia University Press, 1997.

Mann, James. *About Face: A History of America's Curious Relationship with China, from Nixon to Clinton.* New York: Knopf, 1999.

Mao Zedong. "On the Chungking Negotiations." *Selected Works of Mao Tse-tung,* Vol. 4. Peking: Foreign Language Press, 1965.

Nathan, Andrew J., and Kellee S. Tsai. "Factionalism: A New Institutionalist Restatement." *China Journal,* July 1995, pp. 157–192.

Nixon, Richard M. "Asia after Vietnam." *Foreign Affairs,* No. 46, October 1967, pp. 111–125.

——. *RN: The Memoirs of Richard Nixon.* New York: Grosset and Dunlap, 1978.

——. *Leaders.* New York: Warner Books, 1980.

Ogura, Kazuo. "How the 'Inscrutables' Negotiate with the 'Inscrutables': Chinese Negotiating Vis-à-Vis the Japanese." *China Quarterly,* No. 79, September 1979, pp. 529–552.

Oksenberg, Michel. "A Decade of Sino-American Relations." *Foreign Affairs,* Fall 1982, pp. 175–195.

——. *Shaping U.S.-China Relations: A Long-Term Strategy.* New York: Council on Foreign Relations, 1997.

Peng Di. "Confused American 'Strategist.' " *Xin Hua,* December 1, 1980, in *Foreign Broadcast Information Service, PRC,* December 1, 1980.

Pye, Lucian W. *The Spirit of Chinese Politics.* Cambridge, Mass.: M.I.T. Press, 1968.

——. *The Dynamics of Chinese Politics.* Cambridge, Mass.: Oelgeschlager, Gunn & Hain, 1981.

——. *Chinese Commercial Negotiating Style.* Cambridge, Mass.: Oelgeschlager, Gunn & Hain, 1982.

——. *Chinese Negotiating Style: Commercial Approaches and Cultural Principles.* Westport, Conn.: Quorum Books, 1992.

——. "Factions and the Politics of Guanxi: Paradoxes in Chinese Administrative and Political Behavior." *China Journal,* July 1995, pp. 35–54.

Pye, Lucian W., and Nathan Leites. *Nuances in Chinese Political Culture.* P-4504. Santa Monica, Calif.: RAND, November 1970. (Also published in *Asian Survey.*)

Robinson, Thomas W. *The Sino-Soviet Border Dispute: Background, Development, and the 1969 Clashes.* RM-6171-PR. Santa Monica, Calif.: RAND, 1970.

Robinson, Thomas W., and David Shambaugh, eds. *Chinese Foreign Policy: Theory and Practice.* Oxford: Clarendon Press, 1994.

Ross, Robert S. *Negotiating Cooperation: The United States and China 1969–1989.* Stanford, Calif.: Stanford University Press, 1995.

Samuelson, Louis J. *Soviet and Chinese Negotiating Behavior: The Western View.* Beverly Hills, Calif.: Sage, 1976.

Schroeder, Paul E. "The Ohio-Hubei Agreement: Clues to Chinese Negotiating Practice." *China Quarterly,* No. 91, September 1982, pp. 486–491.

Scott, Gary L., and Shinobu Takashi. "Reassessing the Japan-China Peace and Friendship Treaty Negotiations: A Comparative Foreign Policy Perspective." *Journal of Northeast Asian Studies,* Vol. 2, No. 4, December 1983, pp. 51–68.

Shultz, George P. *Turmoil and Triumph.* New York: Scribner's, 1993.

Snow, Edgar. *Red Star over China.* New York: Random House, 1938.

Solomon, Richard H. *Mao's Revolution and the Chinese Political Culture.* Berkeley, Calif.: University of California Press, 1971. Ann Arbor, Mich.: University of Michigan, Center for Chinese Studies, 1999.

——. *The China Factor: Sino-American Relations and the Global Scene.* Englewood Cliffs, N.J.: Prentice-Hall, 1981.

——. *Chinese Political Negotiating Behavior: A Briefing Analysis.* R-3295. Santa Monica, Calif.: RAND, 1985.

Sun Tzu. *The Art of War,* ed. James Clavell. New York: Delta Books, 1983.

Sutter, Robert G. *Shaping China's Future in World Affairs: The Role of the United States.* Boulder, Colo.: Westview Press, 1996.

Swaine, Michael. *The Role of the Chinese Military in National Security Policymaking.* Santa Monica, Calif.: RAND, 1996.

Talbot, Strobe. *Deadly Gambits.* New York: Knopf, 1984.

Tang, Tsou. "Chinese Politics at the Top: Factionalism or Informal Politics? Balance-of-Power Politics or a Game to Win All?" *China Journal,* July 1995, pp. 95–156.

Teiwes, Frederick C. "The Paradoxical Post-Mao Transition: From Obeying the Leader to 'Normal Politics.'" *China Journal,* July 1995, pp. 55–94.

Unger, Jonathan, ed. *Chinese Nationalism.* Armonk, N.Y.: M. E. Sharpe, 1996.

U.S. House, Committee on International Relations, Subcommittee on International Economic Policy and Trade. *The U.S.-China Intellectual Property Rights Agreement: Implications for U.S.-Sino Commercial Relations.* Hearing, March 2, 1995. Washington, D.C.: U.S. Government Printing Office, 1995.

——. *The U.S.-China Intellectual Property Rights Agreement and Related Trade Issues.* Hearing, March 7, 1996. Washington, D.C.: U.S. Government Printing Office, 1997.

U.S. Senate, Committee on Governmental Operations, Subcommittee on National Security and International Operations. *Peking's Approach to Negotiations: Selected Writings.* Washington, D.C.: U.S. Government Printing Office, 1969.

Vance, Cyrus. *Hard Choices: Critical Years in America's Foreign Policy.* New York: Simon and Schuster, 1983.

Vogel, Ezra F., ed. *Living with China: U.S.-China Relations in the Twenty-First Century.* New York: W. W. Norton, 1995.

Wang, Bingnan. "Nine Years of Sino-U.S. Talks in Retrospect." *Guangzhou Ribao,* translated in *Foreign Broadcast Information Service, PRC,* Parts 1–3, October 19, 1984, pp. B3–B7; Parts 4–5, October 25, 1984, pp. B2–B6; Part 6, October 31, 1984, pp. B4–B5.

Weakland, John. "The Organization of Action in Chinese Culture." *Psychiatry,* No. 13, 1950, pp. 361–370.

Whyte, Martin K. *Small Groups and Political Rituals in China.* Berkeley, Calif.: University of California Press, 1974.

Wilhelm, Alfred D., Jr. *The Chinese at the Negotiating Table.* Washington, D.C.: National Defense University, 1994.

Wu, Xiuquan. "January in Kaesong." *Jiefang Jun Wenyi,* translated in *Foreign Broadcast Information Service, PRC,* August 17, 1983, pp. D2–D6.

Young, Kenneth T. *Negotiating with the Chinese Communists: The United States Experience, 1953–1967.* New York: McGraw-Hill, 1968.

Yu, Anthony C. "The Confucian Concept of Order." *Thought,* No. 43, 1968, pp. 249–272.

Zhao, Quansheng. *Interpreting Chinese Foreign Policy: Micro-Macro Linkage Approach.* Hong Kong: Oxford University Press, 1996.

Zhao Ziyang. "Report on the Work of the Government." Delivered to the First Session of the Sixth National People's Congress. *Beijing Review,* No. 27, July 4, 1983.

Zhou Enlai. "Report to the Tenth National Congress of the Chinese Communist Party," August 24, 1973. *Foreign Broadcast Information Service, PRC,* August 31, 1973.

Cross-Cultural Negotiation

Avruch, Kevin. *Culture and Conflict Resolution.* Washington, D.C.: United States Institute of Peace Press, 1998.

Avruch, Kevin, and Peter W. Black, eds. *Conflict Resolution: Cross-Cultural Perspectives.* New York: Greenwood Press, 1991.

Binnendijk, Hans, ed. *National Negotiating Styles.* Washington, D.C.: Center for the Study of Foreign Affairs, 1987.

Blaker, Michael. *Japanese International Negotiating Style.* New York: Columbia University Press, 1977.

Brake, Terence Walker, and Danielle Medina. *Doing Business Internationally: The Guide to Cross-Cultural Success.* Burr Ridge, Ill.: Irwin Professional Publishers, 1995.

Casse, Pierre. *Managing Intercultural Negotiations: Guidelines for Trainers and Negotiators.* Washington, D.C.: SIETAR International, 1985.

Cohen, Raymond. *Negotiating Across Cultures: International Communication in an Interdependent World.* Rev. ed. Washington, D.C.: United States Institute of Peace Press, 1997.

Ellis, Richard J., and Michael Thompson, eds. *Culture Matters: Essays in Honor of Aaron Wildavsky.* Boulder, Colo.: Westview Press, 1997.

Fisher, Glen. *International Negotiation: A Cross-Cultural Perspective.* Chicago: Intercultural Press, 1980.

——. *Mindsets: The Role of Culture and Perception in International Relations.* 2nd ed. Yarmouth, Maine: Intercultural Press, 1997.

——. *The Mindsets Factor in Ethnic Conflict: A Cross-Cultural Agenda.* Yarmouth, Maine: Intercultural Press, 1998.

Fisher, Roger, and William Ury. *Getting to Yes: Negotiating Agreement Without Giving In.* Boston: Houghton Mifflin, 1981.

Hofstede, Geert H. *Cultures and Organizations: Software of the Mind.* London: McGraw-Hill, 1991.

Hudson, Valerie M., ed. *Culture and Foreign Policy.* Boulder, Colo.: Lynne Reinner Publishers, 1997.

Iklé, Fred Charles. *How Nations Negotiate.* New York: Harper and Row, 1964.

Leites, Nathan. *The Operational Code of the Politburo.* New York: McGraw-Hill, 1951.

Schecter, Jerrold L. *Russian Negotiating Behavior: Continuity and Transition.* Washington, D.C.: United States Institute of Peace Press, 1998.

Silkenat, James R., and Jeffrey M. Aresty, eds. *The ABA Guide to International Business Negotiations: A Comparison of Cross-Cultural Issues and Successful Approaches.* Chicago: American Bar Association, 1994.

Storti, Craig. *The Art of Crossing Cultures.* Yarmouth, Maine: Intercultural Press, 1990.

Storti, Craig, with Laurette Bennhold-Samaan. *Culture Matters: The Peace Corps Cross-Cultural Workbook.* Washington, D.C.: Peace Corps Information Collection and Exchange, 1997.

U.S. House, Committee on Foreign Affairs. *Soviet Diplomacy and Negotiating Behavior: Emerging New Context for U.S. Diplomacy.* Washington, D.C.: U.S. Government Printing Office, 1979.

Mao Zedong *(far left)* greets Richard Solomon of the National Security Council staff during a visit to China in 1975. Standing next to Mao is President Gerald Ford and his wife Betty Ford. *(Courtesy Chinese Government)*

Richard H. Solomon is president of the United States Institute of Peace. Prior to joining the Institute in 1993, he served for a dozen years in the U.S. government. His assignments included assistant secretary of state for East Asian and Pacific affairs (1989–92), director of the Policy Planning Staff of the Department of State (1986–89), and U.S. ambassador to the Philippines (1992–93).

Before joining the State Department, Solomon was head of the RAND Corporation's Political Science Department (1976–86), where he directed RAND's research program on international security policy. From 1971 to 1976 he was senior staff member for Asian affairs on the National Security Council, where he was involved in the process of normalizing relations with the People's Republic of China. During this time he made nine official trips to China.

Solomon began his professional career as a professor of political science at the University of Michigan (1966–71), where he taught courses on Chinese politics. He earned his S.B. and Ph.D. degrees at the Massachusetts Institute of Technology, where he majored in chemistry and political science, and he did course work in Chinese history, society, and language at Harvard and Yale. He has published numerous professional articles and six books. The first, *Mao's Revolution and the Chinese Political Culture* (1971, 1999), was based on two years of field research in Taiwan and Hong Kong. Subsequent works include *A Revolution Is Not a Dinner Party* (1976), and *The China Factor* (1981).

United States Institute of Peace

The United States Institute of Peace is an independent, nonpartisan federal institution created by Congress to promote research, education, and training on the peaceful resolution of international conflicts. Established in 1984, the Institute meets its congressional mandate through an array of programs, including research grants, fellowships, professional training programs, conferences and workshops, library services, publications, and other educational activities. The Institute's Board of Directors is appointed by the President of the United States and confirmed by the Senate.